REDESIGNING
**CREATION**
Debating the Biotech Revolution

IDE4S in CONFLICT

# Marnie J. McCuen

ARY McCUEN
**publications inc.**

411 Mallalieu Drive
Hudson, Wisconsin 54016
Phone (715) 386-7113

*illustration and Photo Credits:*

Kitty Kennedy 56, 106; Monsanto 81; Office of Technology Assessment 11; Andrew Singer 28, 126.

© 2000 by Gary E. McCuen Publications, Inc.
411 Mallalieu Drive, Hudson, Wisconsin 54016

(715) 386-7113

International Standard Book Number
0-86596-185-9
Printed in the United States of America

# CONTENTS

Ideas in Conflict

INTRODUCTION

*Chapter 1*  **BIOCAPITALISM: PEOPLE, HEALTH AND THE MARKET**

*Chapter 2*  **BODY FOR SALE**

*Chapter 3*    **FRANKENFOOD OR FUTURE OF
              FARMING?: CROP BIOTECHNOLOGY**

## REASONING SKILL DEVELOPMENT

These activities may be used as individualized study guides for students in libraries and resource centers or as discussion catalysts in small group and classroom discussions.

# IDEAS
# in CONFLICT

This series features ideas in conflict on political, social, and moral issues. It presents counterpoints, debates, opinions, commentary, and analysis for use in libraries and classrooms. Each title in the series uses one or more of the following basic elements:

*Introductions that present an issue overview giving historic background and/or a description of the controversy.*

*Counterpoints and debates carefully chosen from publications, books, and position papers on the political right and left to help librarians and teachers respond to requests that treatment of public issues be fair and balanced.*

*Symposiums and forums that go beyond debates that can polarize and oversimplify. These present commentary from across the political spectrum that reflect how complex issues attract many shades of opinion.*

*A global emphasis with foreign perspectives and surveys on various moral questions and political issues that will help readers to place subject matter in a less culture-bound and ethnocentric frame of reference. In an ever-shrinking and interdependent world, understanding and cooperation are essential. Many issues are global in nature and can be effectively dealt with only by common efforts and international understanding.*

*Reasoning skill study guides and discussion activities provide ready-made tools for helping with critical reading and evaluation of content. The guides and activities deal with one or more of the following:*

RECOGNIZING AUTHOR'S POINT OF VIEW

INTERPRETING EDITORIAL CARTOONS

VALUES IN CONFLICT

WHAT IS EDITORIAL BIAS?

WHAT IS SEX BIAS?

WHAT IS POLITICAL BIAS?

WHAT IS ETHNOCENTRIC BIAS?

WHAT IS RACE BIAS?

WHAT IS RELIGIOUS BIAS?

*From across **the political spectrum** varied sources are presented for research projects and classroom discussions. Diverse opinions in the series come from magazines, newspapers, syndicated columnists, books, political speeches, foreign nations, and position papers by corporations and nonprofit institutions.*

---

### About the Publisher

The late Gary E. McCuen was an editor and publisher of anthologies for libraries and discussion materials for schools and colleges. His publications have specialized in social, moral and political conflict. They include books, pamphlets, cassettes, tabloids, filmstrips and simulation games, most of them created from his many years of experience in teaching and educational publishing.

---

READING **1**

# THE NEW AND OLD BIOTECHNOLOGY

## Union of Concerned Scientists

*The Union of Concerned Scientists (UCS) is a citizen/scientist organization which promotes stewardship of the global environment, renewable energy, sustainable agriculture, and the curtailment of weapons of mass destruction. Contact UCS at Two Brattle Square, Cambridge, MA 02238, United States, (617) 547-5552, www.ucsusa.org/.*

### ■ POINTS TO CONSIDER

1. Summarize UCS' definition of biotechnology. What are the shortcomings of this definition, according to the authors?

2. Discuss some traditional biotechnologies and their applications. According to the article, why are some traditional biotechnologies more effective than the new?

3. Describe some new biotechnologies. What is the difference between gene modification and cloning?

4. Define "novel organism."

5. Contrast gene therapy and genetic enhancement. Think of ethical implications that may arise from both.

NOTE: As you complete the readings in this book, keep in mind the type of biotechnology discussed. Refer back to Reading One for guidance.

*One way of thinking about biotechnology is to consider two categories of activities: those that are traditional and familiar and those that are relatively new.*

Biotechnology is a broad term that applies to all practical uses of living organisms — anything from microorganisms used in the fermentation of beer to the most sophisticated application of gene therapy. The term covers applications that are old and new, familiar and strange, sophisticated and simple.

Defined in this way, the term is almost too broad to be useful. One way of thinking about biotechnology is to consider two categories of activities: those that are traditional and familiar and those that are relatively new. Within each category can be found technologies that are genetic — that involve modifications of traits passed down from one generation to the next — and technologies that are not....

## TRADITIONAL BIOTECHNOLOGIES

A prime example of traditional genetic biotechnologies is selective breeding of plants and animals. The rudiments of selecting plants and animals with desirable traits and breeding them under controlled conditions probably go back to the dawn of civilization, but the expansion of knowledge about genetics and biology in this century has developed selective breeding into a powerful and sophisticated technology. New molecular approaches like marker-assisted breeding (which enhances traditional breeding through knowledge of which cultivars or breeds carry which trait) promise to enhance these approaches even further.

Traditional breeding technologies have been immensely successful, and indeed are largely responsible for the high yields associated with contemporary agriculture. These technologies should not be considered *passé* or out of date. For multigene traits like intrinsic yield and drought resistance, they surpass genetic engineering. This is because selective breeding operates on whole organisms — complete sets of coordinated genes — while genetic engineering is restricted to three or four gene transfers with less control over where the new genes are inserted. For the most important agronomic traits, traditional breeding remains the technology of choice.

Other traditional nongenetic biotechnologies include the fermentation of microorganisms to produce wine, beer, and cheese. Industry also uses microorganisms to produce various products such as enzymes for use in laundry detergents. In an effort to find microorganisms that produce large amounts of enzymes, scientists sometimes treat a batch of organisms with radiation or chemicals to randomly produce genetic alterations. The process, called mutagenesis, produces numerous genetic changes in the bacteria, among which might be a few that produce more of the desired product.

## NEW BIOTECHNOLOGIES

Many new biotechnologies do not involve modifications of traits passed on to the next generation. A good example is monoclonal antibodies (highly specific preparations of antibodies that bind to a single site on a protein), which have many diagnostic applications, including home pregnancy testing kits. Many biotechnology companies are engaged in these sophisticated, but noncontroversial, technologies.

By contrast, mammalian cloning is a new biotechnology that does not involve gene modification, but is nevertheless highly controversial. Cloning reproduces adult mammals by transplanting a nucleus from an adult cell into an egg from which the nucleus has been removed and allowing the egg to develop in a surrogate manner. The resulting individuals are as similar to the adults from which the nuclei were taken as identical twins are to one another. Although this procedure has profound implications for human reproduction, it does not modify specific traits of an individual, but rather transfers a whole nucleus containing a complete set of genetic information.

The new technology that can affect future generations is genetic engineering, a technology based on the artificial manipulation and transfer of genetic material. This technology can move genes and the traits they dictate across natural boundaries — from one type of plant to another, from one type of animal to another, and even from a plant to an animal or from an animal to a plant. Cells modified by these techniques pass the new genes and traits on to their offspring. Genetic engineering can apply to any kind of living organism from microorganisms to humans.

Genetic engineering can be applied to humans to replace or supplement defective genes. Where engineering is intended to

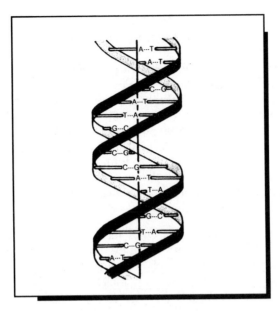

"Structure of DNA," office of Technology Assessment, 1984.

cure disease, it is called gene therapy. Potential applications that are not related to disease, such as the modification of traits like height, are sometimes called genetic enhancement. Currently, most genetic engineering of humans is done on nonreproductive or somatic cells, like those from bone marrow. The effects of this somatic cell gene therapy are confined to the treated individual. By contrast, germ line gene therapy would modify reproductive cells, so that the modification could be passed on to future generations.

## GENETIC ENGINEERING

Genetic engineering refers to a set of technologies that artificially move functional genes across species boundaries to produce *novel organisms*. The techniques involve highly sophisticated *manipulations of genetic material* and other biologically important chemicals.

Genes are special chemicals that work as sets of blueprints to determine an organism's traits. Moving genes from one organism to another moves those traits. Through genetic engineering, genes can be moved across natural boundaries. The resultant organisms

11

# RECOMBINANT DNA

DNA, which takes the structural form of a double-stranded helix, is the information system of living organisms. DNA in all organisms is composed, in part, of four chemical subunits called bases. These four bases — guanine (G), adenine (A), thymine (T), and cytosine (C) — are the coding units of genetic information. These bases normally pair predictably — A with G, and T with C — to form the DNA double helix structure. It is the unique ordering of these bases in the helix that determines the function of a given gene, and the complete blueprint for an organism is coded within its DNA.

In general, recombinant DNA technology works in this sequence: first, donor DNA is cut by restriction enzymes into many fragments, one of which contains the sequence of interest. These different fragments are joined with vector DNA to become recombinant DNA molecules. The recombinant molecules are then introduced into the host; for a variety of reasons, only some host cells will take up the recombinant DNA. After this process, the fraction of host cells that received any recombinant DNA must be identified. This initial selection is often accomplished through the use of antibiotics that kill those host cells that did not receive recombinant molecules.

Finally, the small number of recombinant organisms containing the specific donor DNA fragment of interest must be found. This process is completed *via a* tool that detects the gene or gene product of interest. This tool is called a gene probe. Examples of gene probes include a segment of DNA similar to the gene of interest, but from a different organism; a synthetic fragment of DNA deduced from the protein sequence of a gene product; a piece of RNA; or an antibody that binds to the product of interest.

Once identification and purification of the genetically engineered (recombinant) organism has been achieved, the host population containing the cloned gene can be expanded and the cloned gene used to identify, isolate, and scrutinize scarce biological compounds.

Office of Technology Assessment, **New Developments in Biotechnology: Ownership of Tissues and Cells,** Washington, D.C.: U.S. Government Printing Office, 1987.

can have new combinations of genes — and therefore new combinations of traits — that are not found in nature and, indeed, not possible through natural mechanisms. Such a technology is *radically different* from traditional plant and animal breeding.

Nature can produce organisms with new combinations of genes through sexual reproduction. A brown cow bred to a yellow cow may produce a calf of a completely new color. But reproductive mechanisms limit the number of new combinations. Cows must breed with other cows (or very near relatives). Thus, the set of genes naturally available for reshuffling are those found within cows and their near relatives. A breeder who wants a purple cow would be able to breed toward one only if the necessary purple genes were available somewhere in a cow or a near relative to cows. A genetic engineer has no such restriction. If purple genes are available anywhere in nature — in a sea urchin or an iris — those genes could be used in attempts to produce purple cows. This unprecedented ability to shuffle genes means that genetic engineers can make combinations of genes not found in nature.

## RADICALLY DIFFERENT

Thus, genetic engineering is not a minor extension of existing breeding technologies. It is a radically new technology for altering the traits of living organisms by adding genetic material that has been manipulated outside of cells. Since gene transfer occurs by artificial means without regard to natural boundaries, genetic engineering permits combinations of genes and traits not found in nature. This technology allows scientists to rearrange and modify genetic material before transfer and may one day encompass the routine addition of novel genes that have been wholly synthesized in the laboratory.

Novel organisms may, however, bring novel *risks,* as well as the desired *benefits....*

READING

**2**

# THE FUTURE OF BIOTECHNOLOGY

## Edward T. Shonsey

*Edward T. Shonsey is the President and Chief Executive Officer of Novartis Seeds. His comments were excerpted from a speech before the U.S. Grains Council, Value-Enhanced Grains Conference, 9 February 1999.*

## ■ POINTS TO CONSIDER

1. According to Shonsey, what impact will biotechnology have on human life?

2. Do you agree with the statement "…biotechnology in and of itself is meaningless…unless it can be applied to products and services and techniques which make something — someone better?"

3. How does you believe one should evaluate technology? Write a critique of Shoney's statement.

Excerpted from Edward T. Shonsey, "Biotechnology and Transgenic Products," **Vital Speechs of the Day,** 15 March 1999. Reprinted with permission of the author.

*So let me say again, biotechnology in and of itself is meaningless — just so much baloney — unless it can be applied to products and services and techniques which make some thing — some ONE — better....*

Evolution, by its very nature, is a journey. And evolutionary journeys are more meandering than straight-line — full of stops and starts and places where we sometimes lose our sense of direction and our way....

## EVOLUTION

And when it comes to biotechnology, I don't think you should count on there ever being an end to the evolution — at least not in the lifetime of any of us in this room — for many reasons including cost which will define the competition between such things as chemical synthesis and enzymatic engineering.

What I care more about than "getting to the end of the trait" is the fact that we will never look at the world the same again because of this thing we call biotechnology. This web of enabling technologies — I am firmly convinced — WILL change our health, our diets, our jobs and how we solve the complexities of life, itself....

The opportunities presented by biotechnology and bioinformatics are limitless and far-reaching. They will affect every — EVERY — aspect of your, and my life.

Our nutrition and health will be affected by biotech vaccines and antibody production.

Our environment will be profoundly changed as a result of bio-engineered water utilization by crops, waste reduction in livestock and humans — and reduced groundwater contamination because of biotechnology's ability to create plants which need less fertilizer and chemicals.

In medicine, cholesterol, cancer, heart disease, HIV and genetic diseases will become the beneficiaries of our greater understanding of biotechnology. These benefits rest not only in innovation and miracle cures but also in testing, evaluation and manufacture of these cures.

# POWER AND EXERCISE

Technologies, however, are not value-free, nor are they inevitable. The fact is, technologies are amplifications and extensions of our biological bodies, appendages we create out of the stuff of the Earth to help inflate ourselves so that we might more easily overcome spatial limitations, minimize temporal constraints, and better expropriate and consume the world around us. A bow and arrow is an extension of our throwing arm. Automobiles extend our legs and feet. Computers amplify our memory. Every tool we've ever created represents increments of power, a way to exercise an advantage over the forces of nature and each other. The exercise of that power is never neutral, for in the act of utilizing the power inherent in each new tool we fashion, someone or something in the environment is compromised, diminished, or exploited to enhance or secure our own well-being. The point is, power is never neutral. There are always winners and losers whenever power is applied.

The question, then, that should be asked of any new technology being readied for society is whether the power being exercised is appropriate or inordinate in scale or scope....

Jeremy Rifkin. **The Biotech Century: Harnessing the Gene and Remaking the World.** New York: Jeremy P. Tarcher, 1998.

## PARADIGM SHIFTS

Students coming to our labs for internships are rushing back to their campuses and changing the direction of their majors to make sure that what they are learning WILL prepare them for REAL jobs. That's a paradigm that has already shifted.

And here's another: A lot of the research in biotechnology began in the large pharmaceutical houses. But many are closing up institute shops because promises have far exceeded performance.

And that leaves agriculture — once at the lowest end of the research food chain — to carry the technology forward. And drive our primary — and secondary — markets to understand the profound implications of biotechnology.

We, as an example, have now linked a billion-dollar effort of our ag biotech center to an infectious disease center and a pharmaceutical center plus outside alliances such as Diversa. This will not only produce feed enzymes expressed in corn kernels but will also emphasize the cure and the cause of diseases in seven identified therapeutic areas.

And here's another shift in that paradigm....If you're a cereal manufacturer and you see a market in nutritionally-enhanced products, you must let us know what your needs are. That's what is driving partnerships today....

We will continue to keep our eye on the distant, long-term goal: making this a better world in which to live. A world where no one goes hungry because the farmers in their country can't produce enough food for them to eat. A world where children grow up healthy because they receive their immunizations in their breakfast food. A world where precious natural resources are preserved because we — you and I working together — create new alternative sources of fuel and fiber. That's the ultimate destination in the evolution of biotechnology: a better world in which to live. And that, my friends, is no baloney! Thank you.

## CHAPTER 1

# BIOCAPITALISM: PEOPLE, HEALTH AND THE MARKET

READING

3

# BIORESEARCH: CREATING LIFE-SAVING APPLICATIONS

## Biotechnology Industry Organization

*The Biotechnology Industry Organization (BIO) represents nearly 700 biotechnology companies and others involved in biotechnology research.*

### ■ POINTS TO CONSIDER

1. Describe the structure of genes.

2. List some diseases that might someday be treated by gene therapy. Does the author discuss applications of biotechnology beyond disease treatment?

3. What are some of the ethical dilemmas created by advances in biotechnology?

4. Discuss, generally, the position the industry takes on regulation.

Excerpted from the testimony of the Biotechnology Industry Organization before the U.S. Senate Committee on Labor and Human Resources, 25 July 1996.

**BIO supports science-based regulation that assures the public that products are being developed in a responsible manner.**

All living things are made up of cells programmed by the same basic genetic material called DNA (deoxyribonucleic acid). Each unit of DNA is made up of nucleotides: adenine (A), guanine (G), thymine (T) and cytosine (C), as well as a sugar and a phosphate. The nucleotides pair up into strands that twist together in a spiral structure called a double helix of genetic material. The DNA for humans has approximately three billion of these pairs.

While every cell in an individual organism has the same DNA units, the different segments of DNA coding tell individual cells how to differentiate, that is, to develop into an eye or blood cell, a muscle or skin cell, and so forth. DNA also tells different cells to produce specific proteins, enzymes and other substances that the host organism uses to fight disease or fend off bacterial and viral predators and other threats. Stretches of DNA are organized into sections called genes. It is estimated that humans have between 80 to 100,000 genes.

## HUMAN GENES

In humans, genes are arranged on 23 pairs of chromosomes, located in the cell nucleus. Each chromosome carries thousands of genes. If a sequence of DNA becomes garbled or is mutated when cells divide, the mutation may cause disease. In some cases, such as sickle-cell anemia, a single misplaced nucleotide is enough to cause the disease. Errors or damage to genes are responsible for an estimated 3,000 to 4,000 hereditary diseases, including Huntington's disease, cystic fibrosis and Duchenne's muscular dystrophy. In addition, altered genes are known to increase the risk of developing various cancers, diabetes, and heart disease. In other cases, genes might simply compromise the immune system, or create a hyperactive immune system which turns on the host. Genes are essential, but they can also be lethal. It is important to emphasize that not all diseases are caused by genetic defects, but, for the most part, those that are genetic have not been treatable to date.

Our industry is identifying the billions of base pairs and thousands of genes — the basic script of DNA — and beginning to identify the functions of individual genes. Scientists have identified the function of many specific genetic sequences in different organisms. For example, scientists have identified the specific sequences of genetic information responsible for insulin and human growth hormone.

For many diseases a critical part of the research is identifying the gene which causes, or contributes to, the disease. Once the gene is identified, scientists may determine precisely how it causes, or is related to, the disease. This provides critical information about the pathology of the disease. We might learn, for example, that the gene codes for too much of an enzyme and that this surplus enzyme is the essence of the disease. If this is true, scientists might immediately focus on how to inhibit production of this enzyme. If the gene codes for too little of an enzyme, we might focus on how to supplement the body's production of this enzyme. The ultimate technology for a genetic disease is gene therapy, where researchers — and eventually physicians — actually substitute a non-defective gene for the defective gene.

## PROMISING TECHNOLOGY

Gene therapy is a promising technology that uses genes themselves to correct hereditary genetic disorders. In gene therapy, a faulty or missing gene can be replaced to correct a genetic cause of a disease. Sometimes, in gene therapy, cells are removed from a patient, altered to correct a genetic defect or omission, and put back into the body. Sometimes new cells are introduced to produce needed cell-growth factor or perform a beneficial cellular function. Gene therapy has been used, for example, to treat Severe Combined Immune Deficiency (SCID), commonly known as the "bubble boy disease."

Once scientists have identified a gene involved in a disease, it may be possible to develop a diagnostic test which individuals can use to determine whether they have the gene. Developing a diagnostic tool can be extremely complicated. It may be that the gene has fifty or sixty mutations — or variations — as with the BRCA 1 breast cancer gene — or several hundred with the cystic fibrosis gene — and that there is no simple "yes-or-no" answer regarding the gene. Different mutations may lead to more or less susceptibility to the disease, different symptoms, or different mortality and morbidity rates.

In addition, genes often do not give us unequivocal answers

about a disease. We may find that a given gene substantially elevates an individual's susceptibility to a disease. We might say that the individual has an "80% chance of developing the disease by age 50." The problem is that we do not often know which individuals are in the 80% sample and which are in the 20% sample or why. Providing odds on a disease to a patient is complex information, both emotionally and medically. We will need to devote considerable resources as a society toward ensuring that individuals who take these diagnostic tests are counseled on their meaning.

## GREATER DILEMMAS

The greater dilemma is that we will invariably be able to develop diagnostic tests well before we can develop therapies which will alleviate or prevent the disease. This is both a practical, an emotional, and an ethical dilemma. Individuals may be reluctant to take a genetic test which will give them devastating information about their prospects in life. Those who do use the tests may determine to take drastic actions which might prevent the manifestation of the disease. Others may be able simply to take practical steps which will delay the onset of a disease or detection at an early, treatable stage. Because families share genes, the genetic information regarding one family member may have important implications for another. The potential for misinformation and misinterpretation of the information is substantial.

We understand that it is vital for our industry to participate actively and responsibly in the public debate about our technology. We are acutely aware of the pain and suffering of individuals with diseases and we are committed to develop medicines to help them. As our society discusses the difficult bioethics issues, we must ensure that the research continues. The information which this research provides may be troubling, but ultimately this information gives individuals the power to make choices and to heal ourselves. We should not fear the knowledge which our research will provide. However, we must ensure that this knowledge is utilized for the benefit of humankind.

## REGULATION

BIO supports science-based regulation that assures the public that products are being developed in a responsible manner. While the scientific discoveries that led to biotechnology are just now over 40 years old, the industry itself dates only from the 1970s.

## HOPEFUL GENE THERAPY

Aged brains have been restored to youthful vigor in a gene therapy experiment with monkeys that may soon be tested in humans with Alzheimer's disease, researchers report. Scientists hope the treatment will reinvigorate thinking and memory....

By inserting genes for nerve growth factor, or NGF, into the brain, the cells were revived and restored to nearly full vigor....

The therapy is so promising that the researchers applied in June 1999 to the Food and Drug Administration to test the gene therapy technique in humans with Alzheimer's disease....

Associated Press, "Study: Gene Therapy Restores Aged Brain Cells," **Star Tribune,** 14 September 1999.

Scientists working in the field recognized from its inception that this was indeed a breakthrough technology. Twenty years ago researchers wondered whether their work would pose hazards to human health, and worried over the potential environmental impact of genetically-engineered microorganisms.

They initiated a moratorium on all experimentation until there could be a full debate of the issues. In 1975, following a conference of scientists at the Asilomar Conference Center in California, the U.S. National Institutes for Health (NIH) issued formal guidelines to govern biotechnology research.

Today, all NIH-funded research is required to adhere to the NIH's safety guidelines. All organizations carrying out recombinant DNA research are required to form oversight committees with at least two outside members. These committees review experiments to make sure they are conducted in accordance with the NIH guidelines. The biotechnology industry has supported implementation of the guidelines governing biological research and voluntarily adheres to these safety guidelines.

BIO members work hard to create credible, constructive relationships with the U.S. regulatory agencies that administer a wide-ranging set of rules governing biotechnology products and processes. For example, the Food and Drug Administration (FDA) reviews, tests, and approves biologicals, diagnostics, and drugs used on humans. The FDA also requires the ethical consideration of patients' rights which are of paramount importance during bio-pharmaceutical development. For example, federal regulations require that any patient receiving an experimental therapy must give an informed consent, that is, understand and agree to take the risks involved in a clinical trial or in receiving a product undergoing testing. Further along this line, individual hospital committees (institutional review boards, or IRBs) review experimental protocols to protect the rights of patients.

## MINIMIZING RISK

Such reviews consider minimization of risk to the patient, reasonable risks in relation to the anticipated benefits, assurance that the patient understands the risks involved with the treatment, and adequate provisions for monitoring of data. These procedures are applicable to the clinical development of all new experimental therapies including gene therapies.

There is no doubt that scientific discovery is taking place much faster than a generation ago. But if we continue open and informed discussion and debate about biotechnology, we will resolve any novel policy and ethical issues. Responsible, science-based regulation and increased public awareness will foster new developments in biotechnology that will benefit human health.

READING

**4**

# BIOETHICS: ANTICIPATING THE UNDESIRABLE

## David Shenk

*David Shenk is the author of* Data Smog: Surviving the Information Glut *(Harper Collins, 1997).*

### ■ POINTS TO CONSIDER

1. Define the "new paradigm" created by advances in genetic discovery and application.

2. Describe the tension the author suggests between biotechnology, researchers and ethicists.

3. According to Shenk, biotechnology researchers "are careful to limit their publicly stated goals." What is the motivation for these limits? Evaluate the previous reading in light of this statement.

4. What is "Real Ethik?" Why does the author believe bioethicists should employ this?

5. Discuss the author's view that biotechnology and market incentive may upset egalitarian harmony. What are his and the previous authors' views on regulation?

*While public policy generally arbitrates between individual rights and social responsibilities, genetics raises a new paradigm, a struggle between contemporary humanity and our distant descendants.*

We all want a world without Down's and Alzheimer's and Huntington's. But when the vaccine against these disorders takes the form of genetic knowledge and when that knowledge comes with a sneak preview of the full catalogue of weaknesses in each of us, solutions start to look like potential problems. With the early peek comes a transfer of control from natural law to human law. Can the U.S. Congress (which seems intent on shrinking, not expanding, its dominion) manage this new enlarged sphere of influence? Can the churches or the media or the schools? To mention just one obvious policy implication of this biotechnological leap: The abortion debate, historically an issue in two dimensions: (whether or not individuals should have the right to terminate a pregnancy), suddenly takes on a discomfiting third dimension: Should prospective parents who want a child be allowed to refuse a particular *type* of child?...

## BIOETHICS

Such are some of the specific scenarios now being bandied about by bioethicists, who, because of the Human Genome Project (HGP), are flush with thinking-cap money. Five percent of the project's funds (roughly $100 million over fifteen years) is being dedicated to social and ethical exploration, an allotment that prompted Arthur Caplan, director of the University of Pennsylvania's Center for Bioethics, to celebrate the HGP as the "full-employment act for bioethicists." The Department of Energy, the National Institutes of Health, and the International Human Genome Organization all have committees to study the social and ethical implications of genetic research. Popping up frequently are essays and conferences with titles like "Human Gene Therapy: Why Draw a Line?," "Regulating Reproduction," and "Down the Slippery Slope." While genetic researchers plod along in their methodical dissection of chromosomes, bioethicists are leaping decades ahead, out of necessity. They're trying to foresee what kind of society we're going to be living in when and if the researchers are successful. In Sheraton and Marriott conference halls, they pose the toughest questions they can think of. If a single skin cell can reveal the emotional and physical characteristics of an individual, how are we going to keep such information private? At what level of risk should a patient be informed of the potential future onset of a disease? Will employers be free to hire and fire based on information obtained from their prospective employees' karyotypes? Should a criminal defendant be allowed to use genetic predisposition toward extreme aggressiveness as a legitimate defense, or at least as a mitigating factor in sentencing?[1] Should privately administered genetic tests be regulated for accuracy by the government? (Currently, they are not.) Should private companies be able to patent the gene sequences they discover? Should children of sperm donors have the right to know the identity and genetic history of their biological fathers? The only limitation on the number of important questions seems to be the imagination of the inquirer.

## BOUNDARIES

Most fundamental of all, though, are questions regarding the propriety of futuristic gene-based medical techniques. Suppose for a moment that the power to select on the basis of, and possibly even alter, our genetic code does, as many expect, turn out to be extensive. What sort of boundaries should we set for ourselves? Should infertile couples be allowed to resort to a clone embryo rather than adopt a biological stranger? Should any couple have the right to choose the blond-haired embryo over the brown-haired embryo? Homosexuality over heterosexuality?[2] Should we try to "fix" albinism in the womb or the test tube? Congenital deafness? Baldness? Crooked teeth? What about aortas that if left alone will likely give out after fifty-five years? Should doctors instead pursue a genetic procedure that would give the ill-fated embryo a heart primed for ninety-nine years?

To address these questions, bioethicists need to determine what competing interests are at stake. If a father wants a blue-eyed stout-hearted son and is able to pay for the privilege, which will cause no harm to anyone else, what's the problem? Consider the prospect of a pop-genetics culture in which millions choose the same desirable genes. Thousands of years down the line, the diversity in the human gene pool could be diminished, which any potato farmer can tell you is no way to manage a species. While public policy generally arbitrates between individual rights and social responsibilities, genetics raises a new paradigm, a struggle between contemporary humanity and our distant descendants....

Cartoon by Andrew Singer. Reprinted by permission.

## RESEARCHERS V. ETHICISTS

Nowhere in the [Human Genome] Project summaries will an affiliated researcher be found yearning publicly for a world filled with fat-proof, freezable people (although no one seems to have misgivings about any conceivable genetic engineering of pigs, cows, or other nonhumans). More modestly, the stated hopes for the application of gene mapping include a greater understanding of DNA and all biological organisms; new techniques for battling genetic diseases; a new prevention-oriented type of medicine; and a windfall for agribusiness and other biotech industries.

The fact that researchers are careful to limit their publicly stated goals reflects not so much a deeply ingrained social ethic, says Arthur Caplan, as a canny political awareness. "If uncertainty about what to do with new knowledge in the realm of genetics is a cause for concern in some quarters," he writes in the book *Gene Mapping*, "then those who want to proceed quickly with mapping the genome might find it prudent to simply deny that any application of new knowledge in genetics is imminent or to promise to forbear from any controversial applications of this knowledge...[This] is the simplest strategy if one's aim is not applying new knowledge but merely to be allowed to proceed to acquire it." Caplan thus exposes a built-in tension between researchers and ethicists. Ethicists are paid to arouse concern, but researchers lose funding if too many people get too worried.

Spotlighting the personal motivations of their researcher counterparts might seem a little beyond the purview of bioethicists, but in fact bioethicists are obliged, as part of the exploration of propriety, not only to hope for the ideal social circumstances of genetic engineering but also to consider the more probable landscape for it, an approach we might call *Real Ethik*. To simply declare certain procedures immoral and call for an immediate and permanent ban is to ignore brazenly the history of technology, one lesson of which might fairly be summarized as "If it can be done, it will be done." E.g., the atomic bomb. The genie found its way out of that bottle in short order, almost instantaneously revolutionizing the way we think about conflict. *Real Ethik* dictates that other genies will escape from their bottles no matter what we do to stop them....

## REAL ETHIK

This inescapable element of human nature is why industrialized societies that respect the basic freedoms of their citizens nonetheless impose so many niggling restrictions on them — speed limits, gun control, waste-disposal regulations, food-and-drug preparation guidelines, and so on. As technologies advance further, conferring even more power and choice on the individual — the abilities to travel at astonishing rates of speed, to access and even manipulate vital pieces of information, to blow up huge structures with little expertise — societies will have no option but to guard against new types of abuse. *Real Ethik* is, therefore, inevitably a prescription for aggressive and complex government oversight of society and its powerful new tools.

Scratch the surface of both the information and biotech revolutions, in fact, and what one discovers underneath is a "control revolution," suggests political theorist Andrew Shapiro, a massive transfer of power from bureaucracies to individuals and corporations. In an unregulated control revolution, free markets and consumer choice become even more dominant forces in society than they already are, and in virtually every arena social regulation gives way to economic incentive. Unrestrained consumerism augments the ubiquitousness of pop culture and the free-for-all competition for

## CONSUMER PLAYGROUND

...Making decisions over what genes to insert, recombine, or delete in an effort to "alter," "transform," and "redesign" oneself and one's progeny is less an artistic expression and more a technological prescription. It is not art, but artifice. What some social theorists call the "Creative Age" is really the age of unlimited consumer choice. Unfortunately, we increasingly confuse the ability to choose with the ability to create, especially with regard to the new biotechnologies. Now that we can begin reengineering ourselves, we mistakenly think of the new technological manipulation as a creative act, when in reality it is merely a set of choices purchased in the marketplace....

Jeremy Rifkin, **The Biotech Century: Harnessing the Gene and Remaking the World,** New York: Jeremy P. Tarcher/Putnam, 1998.

scarce resources. Ultimately, even such social intangibles as privacy become commodified.

The unpleasant extremes of this climate are not very difficult to imagine: an over-class buying itself genetic immunity from industrial waste, leaving the working class gasping in its wake; conglomerates encoding corporate signatures onto genetic products, rendering competing products ineffective and enforcing the ultimate brand loyalty; parents resorting to all available legal means to ensure their kids can compete effectively, including attempts to, in the parlance of the Repository for Germinal Choice, "get the best possible start in life." In the absence of legal restrictions, one envisions the development of a free-market eugenic meritocracy — or, to coin a term, "biocapitalism." If left up to the marketplace, designer genes could even allow the wealthy to pass on not only vast fortunes but also superior bioengineered lineages, thereby exacerbating class divisions.

## SURVIVAL OF FREEDOM

With that much freedom and independence, the paradoxical question one must finally ask is: Can freedom and independence, as we know them, survive? The genetic revolution may well deliver the apex of "life, liberty, and the pursuit of happiness," but it seems destined to conflict with another bedrock American principle. Two centuries after it was first proclaimed, we still abide by the conceit — the "self-evident" truth — that "all men are created equal." We know, of course (as did our founding fathers), that this is not literally true: people are born with more, less, and different varieties of strength, beauty, and intelligence. Although we frequently celebrate these differences culturally, from a political and legal standpoint we choose to overlook them. For the purposes of sustaining a peaceful, just, and functional society, we are all considered equal.

An unregulated, unrestricted genetic revolution, by highlighting our physical differences and by allowing us to incorporate them in our structures of enterprise, might well spell the end of this egalitarian harmony. In this pre-genetics era, we are all still external competitors, vying for good jobs, attractive mates, comfortable homes. After the revolution has begun in earnest, much of the competition will likely take place under the skin. We will compete for better code. Such a eugenic culture, even one grounded in a democracy, will inevitably lead to the intensified recognition and exaggeration of certain differences. In a newly human-driven evolution, the differences could become so great that humans will be literally transformed into more than one species. But even if this doesn't happen, our thin metaphysical membrane of human solidarity might easily rupture under the strain. "The mass of mankind has not been born with saddles on their backs," Thomas Jefferson wrote two centuries ago, "nor a favored few booted and spurred, ready to ride them...." Who today can consider the momentum of genetic research and be confident that in another two centuries Jefferson's words will still hold true?

## NOTES FOR READING FOUR

1 This question is not hypothetical in February 1994, Stephen Mobley was convicted of murder and sentenced to death. In their appeal Mobley's lawyers argued that he had inherited a strong predisposition toward aggression. The appeal was rejected. But Deborah Denno, professor of law at Fordham University, believes that genetics evidence will be admitted in U.S. courts within a few years. "Given that so many people who commit homicides also have histories of families with relatives who are also incarcerated," she said in the London Independent, "I think it's just a matter of time before somebody tries it again."

2 Dean Hamer, chief of the National Cancer Institute's gene-structure section, claims to have discovered genetic markers for behaviors such as sexual orientation, thrill seeking, and neurosis. "Psychiatrists making diagnoses and prescribing drugs in the future will look at patients' DNA, just the way they now ask about family history," Hamer has said. Follow-up studies have been inconclusive.

READING

# 5

# FROM BEER TO BIOCHIP: ENHANCED DISEASE SCREENING AND TREATMENT

## Clarisa Long

*Clarisa Long is the Abramson Fellow at the American Enterprise Institute and a research fellow at Harvard University.*

## ■ POINTS TO CONSIDER

1. What is the Human Genome Project?

2. Describe older forms of biotechnology. How do these practices differ from newer methods?

3. In your estimation, account for the consumer distrust of biotechnology cited in Long's article.

4. Discuss some of the applications of biotechnology for medicine and human health.

Excerpted from Clarisa Long, "The Future of Biotechnology," **The American Enterprise,** September/October 1998. Reprinted with permission from **The American Enterprise,** a national magazine of politics, business, and culture.

*Biotechnology research...offers precious insights into the genetic basis of disease.*

We live in the early years of a technological revolution based on advances in molecular biology and genetic engineering. The biotech industry is one of the country's most innovative sectors. The Human Genome Project, a 15-year multinational effort to unravel all the genetic information contained in our cells, is ahead of schedule and under budget....

## PREHISTORIC PRACTICE

Contrary to popular conception, biotechnology is not new. Humans have been genetically manipulating living things to meet their needs since prehistoric times. All over the world for millennia, plants and animals have been selectively bred and microorganisms have been used to make wine, cheese, beer, and bread. Ancient Egyptians applied moldy bread to infected wounds for its healing properties — an early use of penicillin. The beginning of the nineteenth century saw the advent of vaccinations. By the end of the century, microorganisms had been discovered, Mendel's work on genetics had finally achieved recognition, and institutes for exploring biotech processes like fermentation had been established by scientists like Louis Pasteur.

Yet in one poll, roughly 40 percent of those surveyed disapproved of centuries-old techniques of crossbreeding plants when those techniques were described as "biotechnology," and one in five thought such techniques were morally wrong. When the label "biotechnology" was applied to age-old methods of breeding better animals, 62 percent disapproved, and half stated they thought it was immoral. Fully 72 percent of the people surveyed thought they had never eaten a plant produced by crossbreeding — in fact, nearly every fruit and vegetable sold in the grocery store comes from crossbred strains — though nine out of ten of the survey participants said they had a good idea of how food is grown in this country.

From a practical perspective, modern biotechnology differs most from its older forms in the speed with which it can manipulate genetic material. In 1953, James Watson and Francis Crick discovered the double-helical structure of DNA, laying the foundations for modern biotech advances. For the past 25 years, scientists have been able to take individual genes from one organism and insert them into another. They can even take genes from one species and insert them into another.

## PRACTICAL IMPROVEMENTS

Such genetic rearrangements are used to improve the nutrition, taste, and appearance of plants, animals, and other food products. Plants engineered with genes for improved pest resistance or fewer nutritional requirements reduce the need for harsh chemicals, fertilizers, and pesticides. For example, Calgene Corporation's FLAVR SAVR™ tomato is genetically engineered to block an enzyme that would normally cause softening and rotting. As a result, the tomato remains firm in transport to market and can be allowed to ripen on the vine before it is picked. In the environmental arena, organisms can be used to digest pollutants like oil slicks and other hazards. Other genetically engineered microbes are being used in industry to produce new vaccines, solvents, chemical compounds, adhesives, fibers, and lubricants.

Scientists have even been able to create animals that carry pieces of human DNA grafted into their own genetic material. These animals are often breathlessly described as "designer animals." A "designer" cow, for example, can be genetically engineered to secrete into its milk substances normally found only in humans. Such organisms, which run the gamut of species from bacteria to sheep and cows, are used to produce insulin, human growth hormone, and other compounds that previously were prohibitively expensive to synthesize in laboratories. Other genetically engineered animals, such as the Onco-Mouse,™ a mouse with a genetic sequence predisposing it to develop cancer, are used in scientific research.

## REVOLUTIONARY MEDICINE

"Biotechnology is revolutionary in the field of medicine. It uses natural weapons — infection-fighting proteins found in the body and the process of life itself — to bolster the human immune system to fight disease," explains Carl Feldbaum, president of the Biotechnology Industry Organization. The pharmaceutical industry is developing new generations of drugs and vaccines to prevent and treat diseases such as hepatitis B, influenza, anemia, diabetes, heart attacks, human growth hormone deficiency, AIDS-related Kaposi's sarcoma, hairy cell leukemia, and kidney transplant rejection. Genetic tests are being developed for thousands of mutations that cause disease in humans. Biochemical assays are used to screen the public blood supply for HIV and the hepatitis B and C viruses.

In the realm of Big Science, the Human Genome Project is making a detailed map of human DNA. The hereditary instructions contained in DNA guide the development and repair of the body throughout a person's lifetime. The 23 pairs of human chromosomes are estimated to contain anywhere from 50,000 to 100,000 genes, although it appears that only about five percent of these are ever active. This project, guided by the National Institutes of Health, has a three billion dollar budget and is estimated to be completed by 2005. The research surrounding the human genome is important, not just for discovering new genes — that's the easy part — but also for identifying the specific functions of each. Thorough knowledge of the genetic basis for disease can help prevent disease, treat genetic conditions, and identify important new drugs....

## TREATING INCURABLE DISEASE

Biotechnology is giving us the potential to treat previously incurable diseases. The appearance of "superbugs," such as antibiotic-resistant tuberculosis bacilli, and deadly diseases like AIDS are forcing scientists to derive new therapies. Researchers are using the tools of biotechnology to develop faster and more efficient diagnoses and treatment for diseases such as cystic fibrosis, sickle-cell anemia, and diabetes. Gene therapy, which introduces into the relevant tissue working genes to replace damaged or faulty ones, has already successfully provided two young girls with functional adenosine deaminase genes that "turned on" their malfunctioning immune systems, allowing them to lead relatively normal lives. Scientists want to expand gene therapy to treat a host of other life-threatening diseases such as cancer.

Cross-species organ transplantation has the potential to save thousands of lives. Each year, approximately 3,000 Americans die waiting for organ transplants, while another 40,000 are on a waiting list for donors, according to the United Network for Organ Sharing. Scientists are working to alleviate the perpetual shortage of human organs available for transplantation by developing genetically engineered pigs whose organs — heart, liver, lungs, or kidneys — can be transplanted into humans. But there are some troubling medical problems to be overcome first, such as the possibility of infecting patients with viruses native only to pigs. Concerns over such species-jumping viruses — in this case from birds to humans — precipitated the mass slaughter of chickens in Hong Kong in the winter of 1997-98 to prevent spread of the so-called "avian flu." The vaccine designed to combat avian flu was itself a biotech product. It contained a purified, genetically engineered version of a protein called hemagglutinin, a component of the virus. Biotechnology also greatly assists efforts by the Centers for Disease Control to monitor the spread of diseases like influenza and to develop vaccines against them.

## INFORMATION TECHNOLOGY

One of the most exciting frontiers of biotechnology occurs at the junction of the Human Genome Project and information technology. Affymetrix, a firm in Santa Clara, California, has produced a "biochip," or DNA array, called the GeneChip.™ It resembles a silicon chip and has the capacity to analyze thousands of genes at once. Ironically, the technology is ahead of the basic science: Molecular biologists are still working on identifying and providing genes for DNA arrays to analyze. Affymetrix hopes that within the next decade it can use this technology to analyze a patient's genetic risks for dozens of diseases, based on a cell sample. A little further down the road may lie tiny chips implanted in the body to deliver precise amounts of drugs to regulate heart rate and hormone secretion or to control artificial limbs.

Whatever the future of these particular avenues of scientific exploration and discovery, biotechnology will loom large in the coming century. According to Dr. Anthony S. Fauci, director of the National Institute of Allergy and Infectious Diseases, "Biotechnology provides the key to unlocking the mysteries of AIDS, multiple sclerosis, and cystic fibrosis. Using this tool, we will solve the worst diseases we face."...

## PRECIOUS INSIGHTS

Biotechnology research, particularly the Human Genome Project, offers precious insights into the genetic basis of disease. But this scientifically invaluable information has encouraged a purely mechanistic conception of humanity. Genetic knowledge often gives its holders an over-developed sense of fate, as illustrated by Nobel Laureate James Watson, former head of the Center for Human Genome Research at the National Institutes of Health, when he said, "We used to think our fate was in the stars. Now we know, in large measure, our fate is in our genes."...

READING

**6**

# FROM PRIVACY TO PEACE OF MIND: DISEASE SCREENING CONCERNS

### Judy E. Garber, M.D., M.P.H.

*Dr. Judy Garber is an oncologist and clinical cancer geneticist at the Dana Farber Cancer Institute in Boston. She directs the Friends of Dana Farber Cancer Risk and Prevention Clinic, and treats patients at the Breast Center. Garber's research focuses on the clinical effects of genetic testing for hereditary cancer susceptibility.*

### ■ POINTS TO CONSIDER

1. Identify the author's concerns about the impact of genetic screening on patients.

2. How might genetic screening, or fear of it, adversely affect human health? (See the scenario Garber sets up at the beginning of her testimony.)

3. Compare and contrast Garber's view of genetic testing and disease treatment with that of Clarisa Long. (See Reading Five.)

4. Discuss the problems with locating a gene in a particular ethnic group which exposes that group to a higher risk for disease.

5. Genetic testing for certain diseases is currently available on a limited basis. In your estimation, what ethical issues might arise when the mapping of the human genome is complete, or with future use of a Gene Card? (See Reading Five.)

Excerpted from the testimony of Judy Garber, M.D., M.P.H., before the Committee on Labor and Resources of the U.S. Senate, 25 July 1996.

*There is an enormous amount of research to be done to capitalize on the opportunities genetics offers, and I am concerned that we will not be able to avail ourselves of its promise if people are afraid to undergo testing for fear of losing their insurance and employment.*

I ask you to imagine that you are a physician, and the patient you are seeing is a 30-year-old woman paralegal you have seen once before for strep throat. This time she tells you that she is very worried. Her mother died of breast cancer at age 45, when she was 13, so she has always been aware that she would need to start mammograms a little early. But her 33-year-old sister was just diagnosed with breast cancer after the birth of her first child, a girl, and she has now learned that her maternal grandmother had ovarian cancer. She is about to get married, and she proudly tells you that her fiancé has his own business. She has heard that genetic testing for breast cancer susceptibility is available, and tells you that if she has an altered susceptibility gene, she will have her breasts and ovaries removed and adopt children, because she would not want her children to risk growing up without a mother. What should you say?

## A PHYSICIAN'S ADVICE

You can tell her that she is correct that genetic testing for breast and ovarian cancer susceptibility is now available in a limited way, and will be more widely available in the next months and years. You can tell her that this is possible because women from families like hers participated in research over the preceding 25 years that finally gave them a reason for the cancers in their families, and the hope that the information could be used to help their children and grandchildren escape their medical destinies. You can tell her that the medical community hopes very much that scientists will be able to use the power of genetics and the fundamental way it has improved the understanding of cancer and other diseases to design strategies that will improve treatment and prevention. You can tell her that you look forward to a time when the interaction between genes and environment and lifestyle will be understood well enough for you to be able to advise her how to delay or prevent cancer even if she does have an increased risk. It seems so different now to see this woman and realize that it may be possible for her to learn whether or not she shares an altered susceptibility gene and the high risk of cancer of her relatives, or whether she did not inherit the altered gene, and, despite the family history, does not have an 85% lifetime risk of breast cancer, and a 40 to 60% risk of ovarian cancer.

Most of that is in the future, however. As the physician, you do tell your patient that testing is available, and becoming more available. For most women, testing would start with her sister with breast cancer, so that the altered gene in the family could be identified, and a negative test for your patient would be interpretable. If she is found to be free of the altered gene, she would be at usual risk for cancer, and would surely not want to consider the rather radical approach to reducing her risk that she described to you. But what if she were found to have the altered gene? Her fiancé is self-employed, and the legal firm where she works is small. Her altered gene could jeopardize her ability to obtain health insurance, or to change coverage, or to obtain coverage that will permit her to obtain the medical care she will most need. If you help her to be tested anyway, telling her that you will help her to protect the privacy of her test result by recommending that she pay for the test out-of-pocket, what will you do with the results? Should you write them in the medical record where they could be inadvertently discovered by another provider or insurer? When you refer her to a gynecologist for close monitoring, what do you write in the letter? What if the gynecologist is uncomfortable not recording the test results? The quality of testing is not closely regulated — can you imagine an error in this test result?

What if she decides that the risk of losing insurance is too great, and that she will deal with this by having her breasts and ovaries removed before cancer develops? When the surgeon applies for prior approval for the mastectomies and reconstructions, rather costly procedures that are unlikely to completely eliminate cancer risk and are without proven efficacy even in reducing risk, what if the insurer declines to pay unless the patient has testing and is found to have the gene? What happens to her right to decide for herself what she want to know?

## OPPORTUNITY AND APPREHENSION

I believe that genetics offers incredible opportunity, the promise of fundamentally changing the way we treat cancer, and the strategies by which we may prevent it. Perhaps people with particular hereditary forms of cancer should be treated differently

## POSSIBLE GUIDELINES

...1) Every genetic decision is unique, based on individual responses to risk and uncertainty in the context of personal values and circumstances.

2) The consequences of genetic decisions are not confined to individuals, but may affect family members directly and society indirectly.

3) Advances in the diagnosis and treatment of genetic disorders may rapidly change perceptions of what counts as a genetic disease or disability....

Mary Terrell White, "Making Responsible Decisions," **Hastings Center Report**, vol. 29, no. 1, January/February 1999.

because their tumors are fundamentally different in the way they handle specific chemotherapeutic agents. If strategies can be found to prevent or at least significantly delay the onset of breast cancer, for example, in individuals at markedly increased risk based on inherited susceptibility, those same strategies might prevent or delay breast cancer in most women, who have a significant lifetime risk of breast cancer development for unclear reasons.

There is an enormous amount of research to be done to capitalize on the opportunities genetics offers, and I am concerned that we will not be able to avail ourselves of its promise if people are afraid to undergo testing for fear of losing their insurance and employment. There are many other reasons people do not wish to look into the crystal ball, including anxiety, concerns about altering family relationships, and the very real fact that for most, but not all hereditary susceptibilities, there are not yet proven effective strategies to reduce risks should they be found to have altered genes. Some risk education strategies have been known to be effective — like colonoscopies and polypectomies and particular medications in Hereditary Non-Polyposis Colon Cancer (HNPCC) families, and we should expect more. There are concerns about testing of children, where the benefits of avoiding disease might be greatest, but the risks of psychological harm to patients and families are also of great concern. Will parents treat their children differently if they know they may develop cancer in childhood or early adulthood? How will the children perceive themselves, and their futures? These are very important human issues, and they may be unavoidable. Insurance discrimination, employment discrimination and even education discrimination are avoidable.

## ETHNIC GROUPS

I would like to speak briefly as a member of a breast cancer family. My mother had breast cancer in her 40's and fortunately survives 30 years later. Three of her close relatives have also had breast cancer, and her sister had a related malignancy. I have a wonderful husband, and my brother and I each have a daughter, and there are other girls in the next generation. My family is of Ashkenazi Jewish descent, and you may be aware that the prevalence of particular alterations in breast and ovarian cancer susceptibility genes have been shown to be increased in this ethnic group. This particular finding could make it possible for me and my family to be more easily and cheaply tested for hereditary cancer susceptibility. In fact, the finding makes it technically possible to screen member of this ethnic group without family history to identify women at increased risk. In Boston, there has not been a huge amount of interest in testing in the Jewish community. There has been great concern about discrimination of all types, and there is some reluctance to participate in research because privacy cannot be protected. I will not tell you what my family is doing with the options available to us now, but I will tell you that I sincerely hope that my daughter will have much more information with which to make decisions in the next 15 to 20 years, and if that information is not available because we as a society could not find ways to protect privacy and facilitate research, I will be very disappointed.

READING

# 7

# CLONING HUMANS:
# PROMISES AND PROBLEMS

## Ezekiel J. Emanuel, M.D., Ph.D.

*Dr. Ezekiel Emanuel is a member of the United States Bioethics Advisory Commission. He specializes in oncology and is an Associate Professor of Medical Ethics and Medicine at Harvard Medical School.*

## ■ POINTS TO CONSIDER

1. Identify another term for "cloning."

2. Summarize and discuss the two arguments for human cloning that Emanuel delineates.

3. Summarize and discuss the three arguments against cloning.

4. Create a unique argument supporting or opposing human cloning.

5. Compare the ethical considerations of human cloning to those of other applications of biotechnology discussed in this chapter.

Excerpted from the testimony of Ezekiel Emanuel before the Subcommittee on Public Health and Safety of the U.S. Senate Committee on Labor and Human Resources, 17 June 1997.

*There may be some circumstances to use somatic cell nuclear transfer technology so compelling that they should be permitted despite objections. Those opposed to cloning of human beings raise concerns about the use of cloning for eugenics, the transgression of moral boundaries as humans try to become God-like, and the inappropriate use of scarce resources.*

There are two main arguments in favor of using somatic cell nuclear transfer technology to clone human beings. The first argument appeals to the right to reproductive liberty. The argument proceeds in five steps:

## PERSONAL CHOICE

Individual autonomy is a core value. Society believes individuals should be free to pursue their own life plans and ideas of personal fulfillment.

Personal choices about reproduction are an essential aspect of individual autonomy. Not only are choices about reproduction intensely personal, they are of critical importance to a person's identity and constitutive of a meaningful and fulfilling life.

Because of the central importance of reproduction to autonomy, American society recognizes a person's right to reproductive liberty, to not having the state interfere with individual reproductive choices. Thus, we recognize an individual's right not to reproduce through the use of contraceptives as well as the right to use reproductive technologies such as artificial insemination and *in vitro* fertilization.

Somatic cell nuclear transfer technology is simply another mechanism for reproduction. To respect autonomy and the right to reproductive liberty, we should permit individuals to decide whether to bear a child using somatic cell nuclear transfer technology or not, just as they can decide whether to use *in vitro* fertilization or not.

While individual autonomy and the particular right to reproductive liberty are neither absolute nor unlimited, they are so fundamental that they can be limited only for compelling reasons, such as serious harms to third parties. Since there are no serious harms to third parties from cloning human beings, and what harms may

44

exist are too speculative and unproven, cloning should be permitted.

## QUALITATIVE DIFFERENCE

Those opposed to cloning reject this analysis by arguing that cloning is qualitatively different from other reproductive technologies and not encompassed by the right to reproductive liberty. Cloning is asexual; it does not involve an exchange of genes or participation by males and females, and therefore is more like replicating a copy of what exists than creating a new being from the contributions of two humans. Further, it is argued that with cloning what is claimed is not a right to reproduce but a right to create a child with a specific genetic endowment. Cloning is less about the meaning and fulfillment of one's own life and more about controlling the nature and characteristics of another human being. Controlling others is not a right that should be respected; the good of the child also needs consideration.

## FOR SCIENCE

The second main argument in favor of cloning human beings is the right to scientific inquiry. Freedom of scientific inquiry is an important value both intrinsically, for its own sake, and instrumentally, for the benefits it produces. But science is not amoral; it must be conducted within ethical limits. We have recognized this by the codes of conduct for biomedical research such as the Nuremberg Code and the Declaration of Helsinki. We also recognize that clinical research must be conducted in accord with the norms of informed consent and after Institutional Review Board (IRB) review. Therefore, the right to scientific inquiry is not absolute; various experiments and techniques can be regulated not to limit knowledge, but to protect the well-being of individuals and other public interests. If the government deemed the harms from somatic cell nuclear transfer technology to be sufficiently compelling, scientific inquiry could be regulated and even restricted.

Ethical arguments against cloning of human beings [fall] into three types, those related to 1) physical harms, 2) psychological harms to the child, and 3) harms to shared social understandings and values.

# PHYSICAL DANGER

Those opposed to cloning of human beings contend that the scientific progress on somatic cell nuclear transfer technology is too immature and the data suggests that cloning of human beings would be physically dangerous. We have had only one successful cloning of a mammalian somatic cell nucleus and hundreds of failures in sheep and other mammals, such as mice. Further, there are other potential risks about which we have limited information: 1) cumulative nuclear mutations that may lead to cancer, deformities, and other diseases in the offspring, 2) premature aging of the clone since normal cells have a defined number of cell divisions before they senesce, and other potential risks to normal development. We would never consider using a novel anti-cancer drug or surgical procedure on human beings after one success in animals when it has such risks and scientific uncertainty; we would demand significantly more cellular and animal research before applying such interventions on humans. The requirement for proven safety and effectiveness is even greater in the case of cloning of human beings because there is no life-threatening or other illness being treated. The physical risks arise only from applying the therapy itself. The Commission believes the known risks based on Dolly, the uncertainty about effectiveness and safety, and the lack of an illness in need of treatment make attempts at cloning of human beings at this time unethical.

# QUALITY OF SEPARATENESS

Second, while advocates argue cloning would enhance the autonomy of parents, opponents worry that cloning would undermine the autonomy and individuality of children. Here the worry is about the internal experience of the children who would result from somatic cell nuclear transfer. The philosopher Hans Jonas has said that people have a right to be ignorant of their future, ignorant of the effect of their genome on their character and choices. Joel Feinberg, a legal scholar, put it in terms of having a right to an "open future" and being able to construct one's own life without it being previously laid out. The philosopher Martha Nussbaum argues that one of the ten essential human functional capacities that need protection to ensure that each human being can choose and live a good human life is the quality of "separateness." Separateness means "being able to live one's own life and nobody else's; being able to live one's own life in one's very own surroundings and context and proceeding on a separate path through the world from birth to death." Without such "separateness" or "open future" a life would be seriously lacking in humanness. Combining sperm and eggs to reproduce is a reminder that children replicate neither father nor mother; their genetic uniqueness signifies and reminds us that they are independent beings who need to lead their own lives. The worry is that having the identical genetic endowment as someone who has already existed and lived a life would rob a cloned child of this "separateness." Cloned children would feel that their life is lived under a shadow, as if it has already been lived and played out by another, that one's fate is already determined, that one's choices would not really be free or one's own but imitations of the person who lived before.

Some argue this threat to individuality is based on crude genetic determinism, the false belief that we are totally constituted by our genes. Everyone agrees that while genes are not fully determinative, a person's development and character is shaped by a combination of genetic and environmental influences. More importantly, opponents say that the truth of genetic determinism is not at issue; what is critical is whether the cloned person perceives — and other people behave as if — his or her future is significantly determined by the previously existing person. Carrying the identical genes of another person who already lived, a cloned child's internal experience may be one of being robbed of individuality, separateness and autonomy. Ultimately, it may be Emerson, America's greatest philosopher, who got it right when he said, "One of you is enough."

## DISTURBING THE FABRIC

A third worry raised by opponents is that cloning will undermine a complex web of social understandings and values at the heart of cherishing children. One effect of cloning may be for parents and society to view children as objects and things. When we speak of using people as things we generally have in mind two distinct actions. First, the person is made to serve someone else's goal or purpose; the person is used as a means to my ends and aims rather than his or her own ends. The person becomes the object of someone else's will. Second, the person ceases to be valued intrinsically, but the person's worth is determined by whether he or she possesses certain desirable characteristics. We evaluate material things, like cars and computers, by whether they have certain characteristics and meet specific performance standards.

Unlike genetic screening that is used to prevent a terrible illness, somatic cell nuclear transfer is not done for any purported benefit of the child. Cloning would be done to satisfy the vanity of the nucleus donor or to serve the needs of someone else, such as a dying child in need of a bone marrow donor. In such cases, the child becomes an object, the means for the satisfaction of the wants of the person or couple who uses cloning. In addition, the rationale for using cloning, rather than other forms of reproduction, are to make the cloned child have very specific characteristics. The cloned child is supposed to be like a beloved child that died, or to be a genetic match for an organ transplant, or to express the mathematical or musical qualities of an exceptional person. Because the environment affects the ultimate make-up of a child, a cloned child may not necessarily achieve these standards. Nevertheless, the reasons the person or couple opted for somatic cell nuclear transfer was to create a child with specific characteristics, and the value of the child to them will depend upon meeting or expressing the desired characteristics and qualities. This is why some people worry that cloning would turn procreation and begetting into the making and manufacturing of children, that the humanity and dignity of children will be less respected, that children will be valued instrumentally rather than intrinsically.

## HEALTHY PARENTING

Finally, opponents are concerned that permitting somatic cell nuclear transfer would affect not only how cloned children are treated and valued but the social understanding and norms surrounding family and parenting. Essential to good parenting and healthy families that contribute to the development of flourishing children are certain values — unconditional love, acceptance, openness, security, respect, recognition of individuality, etc. Cloning emphasizes and legitimates maximal parental control over the child; indeed, for its proponents, one of cloning's virtues is granting parents as much control over the type of child they produce as possible. By endorsing parental control and treating the child as an object, cloning of human beings undermines the essential values of good parenting and families — especially unconditional love and acceptance, and respect for individuality — and legitimizes a type of parenting that is usually condemned as overbearing and oppressive.

This effect on the integrity of the family would be exacerbated

## CATHOLIC AND JEWISH PERSPECTIVES

The Catholic Church strongly opposes the taking of human life through abortion, euthanasia or destructive experiments on human embryos.

At first glance, human cloning may not seem to belong on this list. It is presented as a means for creating life, not destroying it. Yet it shows disrespect toward human life in the very act of generating it. Cloning completely divorces human reproduction from the context of a loving union between man and woman, producing children with no "parents" in the ordinary sense. Here human life does not arise from an act of love, but is manufactured to predetermined specifications. A developing human being is treated as an object, not as an individual with his or her own identity and rights.

From a Jewish perspective, cloning is no different than any other technology, in that all the tools of nature were given by G-d to human beings to provide appropriate stewardship. Far from a concern that we are playing G-d in manipulating nature in general and creation of life technology specifically, one of the highest accolades that Judaism grants to a human being is to be called "a partner with G-d in the works of creation."

Excerpted from the testimonies of Cardinal William Keeler and Rabbi Barry Freundel before the Subcommittee on Health and Environment of the U.S. House of Representatives Committee on Commerce, 12 February 1998.

because cloning would separate the genetic, gestational, and rearing parents of a child. The rearing father could be the genetic brother, with the rearing grandparents of a child being the genetic parents. Expectations about the obligations that the parties should assume, and society should morally expect and legally impose, would be uncertain. And, as we have seen with stored embryos, if conflicts develop — the parent rejects the cloned child or a divorce occurs — these uncertainties could become serious problems. Not only could this create legal difficulties but also confused relationships and uncertain duties could undermine a child's sense of security and belonging.

# CONCLUSIONS

There are other arguments for and against cloning of human beings. For instance, there may be some circumstances to use somatic cell nuclear transfer technology so compelling that they should be permitted despite objections. Proponents also point out that most of the objections are speculative and unproven and should not prevent a technique protected as a fundamental right and beneficial to individuals. Those opposed to cloning of human beings raise concerns about the use of cloning for eugenics, the transgression of moral boundaries as humans try to become God-like, and the inappropriate use of scarce resources.

# EXAMINING COUNTERPOINTS

*This activity may be used as an individualized study guide for students in libraries and resource centers or as a discussion catalyst in small group and classroom discussions.*

Scientific secrets long hidden within the complexity of deoxyribonucleic acid, or DNA, are beginning to surface with the mapping of our genetic makeup. We peer into an unknown, desperate for answers to the mysteries of our purpose, evolution and the biological patterns of everything from diseases to psychopathic behavior. The promises and perils look much like an ethical rose bush, delicate roses enshrouded in barbed limbs. As a people we must decide whether the consequences of pushing the barbed limbs aside to research the tantalizing roses is worth the unimaginable risks. As advances in the biotechnological revolution race at us, we must pause and ask, are we ready? Are we ready for the parental choices in aborting a fetus because we know it's predisposed to acne, clumsiness and an average IQ? Are we ready as a society for the day when each of us carries a compact disc with our entire genome bound up in its binary code, for all to scrutinize? Are we ready for private corporations to own the genetic makeup of an entire population, for example, the current ownership of Iceland's genetic makeup? Are we ready for Alzheimer's disease, cancer, multiple sclerosis and countless other diseases that have ravaged humanity for decades to disappear? Are we ready for the biotech world?

– Erik M. Dahl

## The Point:

Biotechnology is a dangerous meddling with the building blocks of life. The Perils far outweigh the Promises of a genetically enhanced world where disease has vanished and everyone is closer to an ambiguous genetic perfection. The Perils include a world turned upside down from the genetic manipulation of a germ into a super-germ, or the eugenic philosophy of molding the human race into an unknown ideal by eliminating all imperfections that don't fit the subjective idea of perfection. A brave new world of transgenic plants, animals and people — where a corporation decides what is the paramount mutation for each species and what mutations should be discarded. In the future we could live in a biotech world where some can't obtain insurance, because their genome shows that they are predisposed to take interest in extreme sports. Soon we will live in a biotech world where nothing is good enough, where everything is less than perfection.

## The Counterpoint:

Biotechnology is a wonderful endeavor that all of humanity will profit from. Someday we will live in a world with no disease, no sickness, no crime, no pain, and maybe even no death. We will cure any undesirable traits and feed the world with super-fruits-vegetables-grains-and-animals. Biotechnology will alleviate the imperfections in the world unlike any previous discovery.

### Guidelines:

For this study, conduct some brief research (i.e., through the World Wide Web, or through gathering past newspaper or magazine articles) before examining the point and counterpoint. Next examine the point and counterpoint and critique each view.

### Questions:

1. Do you agree with the Point or Counterpoint? Explain.
2. Which reading in the book best illustrates the Point?
3. Which reading in the book best illustrates the Counterpoint?
4. Would you like your or your family's entire genome on a CD? Why?
5. What is the perfect human? Why? Compare your answers with those of other students. Are they similar or different? Why?
6. What is eugenics? Do some quick research on the topic. Describe the eugenics movements in North America and Europe in the late nineteenth and twentieth centuries.
7. What are your feelings about past eugenics movements? Does the new biotech age resemble past eugenics movements in your estimation?

## CHAPTER 2

# BODY FOR SALE

READING

# 8

# *HOMO ECONOMICUS:*
## CONSIDERATIONS IN THE COMMERCIALIZATION OF BODY TISSUE

### Dorothy Nelkin and Lori Andrews

*Dorothy Nelkin holds a University Professorship, teaching in the Department of Sociology and the School of Law at New York University. She is a member of the National Academy of Sciences' Institute of Medicine, and co-author of* The DNA Mystique: The Gene as Cultural Icon. *Lori Andrews is Professor of Law at Chicago-Kent College of Law and Director of the Institute of Science, Law and Technology at Illinois Institute of Technology. She is also author of* The Clone Age: Adventures in the New World of Reproductive Technology. *The following is from a forthcoming book by Nelkin and Andrews,* The Business of Bodies: The Value of Body Tissue in the Biotechnology Age.

■ **POINTS TO CONSIDER**

1. What is the significance of the *Moore* decision?

2. Evaluate the concerns of indigenous groups regarding the mapping of their genome sequences.

3. Discuss the implications of biocapitalism for the doctor-patient relationship.

4. How have market incentives changed the language of scientific literature, according to the authors?

Excerpted from Dorothy Nelkin and Lori Andrews, *"Homo Economicus: Commercialization of Body Tissue in the Age of Biotechnology,"* **Hastings Center Report,** vol. 28, no. 5, September/October 1998. Reproduced by permission, The Hastings Center, Dorothy Nelkin, Lori Andrews.

*The body, of course, has long been exploited as a commercial and marketable entity...Yet there is something strange and troubling about the traffic in body tissue, the banking of human cells, the patenting of genes.*

In recent years, biotechnology techniques have transformed a variety of human body tissue into valuable and marketable research materials and clinical products. Blood can serve as the basis for immortalized cell lines for biological studies and the development of pharmaceutical products; the American Tissue Culture Catalogue lists thousands of people's cell lines that are available for sale. Snippets of foreskin are used for the development of artificial skin. Biopsied tissue is used to manufacture therapeutic quantities of genetic material....

## TRAFFIC IN BODY TISSUE

Physicians who treat families with genetic disease are approaching geneticists and offering to "sell you my families"[1] — meaning that they will, for a fee, give the researcher their patients' blood samples. Scientists who isolate certain genes are then patenting them and profiting from their use in genetic tests. Hospitals in Great Britain and Russia sell tissue in order to augment their limited budgets. Between 1976 and 1993, Merieux UK collected 360 tons of placental tissue each year from 282 British hospitals and sent them to France for use in manufacturing drugs.[2] Human tissue has become so valuable that it is sometimes a target for corporate espionage and theft.

In the United States the potential for commercial gain from the body grew as a consequence of legislative measures that were enacted in the 1980s to encourage the commercial development of government-funded research.[3] Legislation allowed universities and nonprofit institutions to apply for patents on federally funded projects and also provided tax incentives to companies investing in academic research. At the same time, changes in patent law turned commercial attention toward research in genetics. A landmark U.S. Supreme Court case in 1980 granted a patent on a life form — *bacterium* — setting the stage for the patenting of human genes.[4]...

Today, joint ventures between industry and universities are thriving, and research scientists are increasingly tied to commer-

55

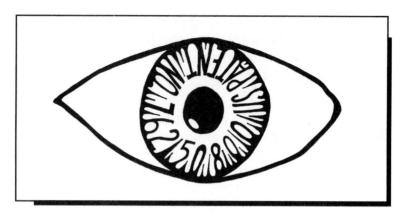

Illustration by Kitty Kennedy. Reprinted with permission.

cial goals....And scientists, hospitals, and universities are patenting genes. The body, of course, has long been exploited as a commercial and marketable entity, as athletes, models, prostitutes, surrogate mothers, and beauty queens are well aware. Yet there is something strange and troubling about the traffic in body tissue, the banking of human cells, the patenting of genes....

## OWNERSHIP OF BODY

John Moore, a patient with hairy cell leukemia, had his spleen removed at the University of California, Los Angeles School of Medicine in 1976. His physician, Dr. David W. Golde, patented certain chemicals in Moore's blood purportedly without his knowledge or consent and set up contracts with a Boston company, negotiating shares worth three million dollars. Sandoz, the Swiss pharmaceutical company, paid a reported fifteen million dollars for the right to develop the Mo cell line....

But Moore felt that his integrity was violated, his body exploited, and his tissue turned into a product: "My doctors are claiming that my humanity, my genetic essence, is their invention and their property. They view me as a mine from which to extract biological material. I was harvested."[5]

The court held that clinicians must inform patients in advance of surgical procedures that their tissue could be used for research, but it denied Moore's claim that he owned his tissue. Who then should reap the *profits* from parts taken from an individual's body? The court decided that the doctor and biotechnology company rather than the patient should profit. The decision rested on the promise of biotechnology innovation. The court did not want to slow down research by "threaten[ing] with disabling civil liability innocent parties who are engaged in socially useful activities, such as researchers who have no reason to believe that their use of a particular cell sample is against a donor's wishes." The court was concerned that giving Moore a property right to his tissue would "destroy the economic incentive to conduct important medical research."[6]...

The privileging of biotechnology companies encouraged a genetics gold rush. In 1992 Craig Venter, a molecular biologist, left the National Institutes of Health to form The Institute for Genomic Research (TIGR), where he compiled the world's largest human gene data bank containing at least 150,000 fragments of DNA sequences. The Institute for Genomic Research was initially funded by a $70 million grant from a firm, Human Genome Services (HGS). Two months after the agreement, HGS contracted with SmithKline Beecham, which gained an exclusive stake in the database with first rights on patentable discoveries....

## INDIGENOUS POPULATIONS

Because people from isolated populations may have unique body tissue, western geneticists, biotechnology companies, and researchers from the Human Genome Diversity Project (HGDP) are seeking blood and hair samples from indigenous groups throughout the world. Their goals are to find disease genes by identifying families with a high rate of genetically linked conditions; to develop genetic tests and therapeutic products; and to "immortalize" the DNA from "vanishing populations."[7]...

The HGDP has confronted angry opposition. Indigenous groups view the taking of their tissue as exploitation. They have accused the program of violating community values, "biopiracy" or "biocolonialism," one more effort to divide their social world. A representative of an indigenous group opined, "You've taken our land, our language, our culture, and even our children. Are you now saying you want to take part of our bodies as well?"[8]...

Indigenous groups also question the relevance of the scientific work to their own health needs, which have less to do with genetic disease than with common disorders such as diarrhea. They argue that DNA is collected, often without adequate knowledge or consent, and then used for products relevant only in wealthy

57

nations. And Native Americans suspect that genetic data will be used against them: just as criteria of blood *quanta* were used to define political entitlements to land and social services, so DNA could be used to override long-standing social relationships. Thus in 1993 the World Council of Indigenous Peoples unanimously voted to "categorically reject and condemn the Human Genome Diversity Project as it applies to our rights, lives, and dignity."[9]...

## THEFT

Products that attain commercial value are inevitably subject to theft, a not uncommon form of redistribution. The traffic in body parts has persisted, spurred as in the nineteenth century, by a shortage of organs and tissue. Body parts have been bought from coroners, stolen from the site of accidents, and sold to meet the demands of industry and medicine.[10] Today, cell lines are a target for international espionage.[11] In a sting operation, agents of the Food and Drug Administration posed as representatives of a tissue bank and ordered tissue from a California dentist who tried to sell them body parts at a discount.[12] In France, a government investigation exposed am embezzlement scheme in which private companies billed local hospitals for synthetic ligament tissue that, it turned out, came from human tissue, which in France cannot legally be bought and sold.[13]...

Demands for spare embryos have also led to undercover redistribution in the *in vitro* fertilization business. At the University of California at Irvine, over 75 couples were affected by theft of eggs and embryos at the University clinic where Dr. Ricardo Asch had apparently been secretly selling some of the eggs extracted from his infertility patients to other patients who were duped into thinking they were from legitimate donors. More than forty civil lawsuits were filed. In July 1997 the University agreed to pay fourteen million dollars to seventy-five couples; two dozen lawsuits still remain. Embryo theft was "predictable, almost inevitable," says Boston University health law professor George Annas. "The field [of *in vitro* fertilization] is so lucrative and so unregulated that someone was just bound to do it."[14]

## BUSINESS OF BODIES

References to body parts in the medical and scientific literature increasingly employ a language of commerce — of banking, investment, insurance, compensation, and patenting. Gene

## ICELAND, BLOOD AND SCIENCE

...Consider Iceland's recent national decision to allow its generations of genealogical data (and practices) and vast stores of medical information to be licensed to deCode Genetics for the purpose of gene discovery. After a broad-based public debate, employing democratic institutions including a free press and independent legislature, the country imposed limits on this new biomedical effort. Although the medical records and genealogical information will be turned over (under a system in which individual identities are to be concealed by encryption) on the basis of presumed consent, the collection of genetic information from volunteers will be constrained by the principle of research-subject self-determination, allowing individuals to withdraw from participation at any time. The licensee is legally liable for misuse of the newly created data base....

Paul R. Billings, "Iceland, Blood and Science," **American Scientists,** May-June 1999.

sequences are patented; cord blood is a "hot property," the body is a "medical factory." Companies "target" appropriate markets for their products. Pathology organizations lobby the government to allow them to use stored tissue samples without consent, for they view such samples as "treasure troves" or "national resources" for research. Geneticists talk of "prospecting" for genes. The body is a "project" — a system that can be divided and dissected down to the molecular level. In a striking statement in the *Moore* case, the defendant, UCLA, claimed that even if Moore's cells were his property, as a state university it had a right to take the cells under "eminent domain."

The body tissue disputes we have described — over the ownership, collection, and distribution of body tissue — raise questions about the assumptions underlying this language of commerce. Who will profit? Who will lose? How will exploitation be avoided? They reflect conflicting beliefs about the body. Is body tissue to be defined as waste, like the material in a hospital bed pan? Is it refuse that is freely available as raw material for commercial products? Or does body tissue have inherent value as part of a person? Are genes the essence of an individual and a sacred part of the human inheritance? Or are they, as a director of SmithKline Beecham purportedly claimed, "the currency of the future."[15]...

The business of bodies may also intrude on the privacy of individuals. Body tissue in the age of biotechnology is a source of valued information. The cord blood banked and the tissue collected from indigenous groups can yield not only research materials, but also information about biological relationships and future genetic conditions. Body tissue can be used to identify the genetic predispositions of individuals (of interest to insurers), to redefine political entitlements (as Native Americans fear), or to reinforce social stereotypes (for example, through research on race and genes for aggression).[16]...

## IMPLICATIONS FOR SCIENCE

The business of bodies affects the fiduciary relationship between doctors and patients. Medical research and clinical practice are ideally considered distinct from the motives of the market. We are leery of scientists who have profit motives in the outcomes of their research or clinicians who have economic interests in particular procedures. Yet a 1996 study of 789 biomedical papers published by academic scientists in Massachusetts found that in 34 percent, one or more authors stood to make money from the results they were reporting.[17] This was because they either held a patent or were an officer or advisor of a biotech firm exploiting the research. In *none* of the articles was this financial interest disclosed.

Patenting in biomedicine hardly enhances trust. Nor does it necessarily encourage the best research. Though considered essential to protect discoveries and provide incentives for investment in research, patenting may actually impede research. Surveys find that patenting has led to reductions in openness and data sharing, delays in publication, and tendencies to select research projects of short-term commercial interest.[18] In several cases, corporations with vested interests have tried to suppress the publications of research findings that were not in their interests. Strains over conflicting commitments have caused some researchers to sever their commercial ties. In June 1997 genetics researcher Craig Venter separated from Human Genome Sciences, giving up a promised 38 million dollars in order to obtain his intellectual freedom.[19] He said the move was prompted by company pressure to delay publication of his results and to influence his scientific findings. He has since joined another commercial venture....

## PATIENT TREATMENT

Moreover, commercialization of body parts may prevent patients from obtaining appropriate health care services by obstructing the distribution of research benefits. Patent rights allow the researcher who identifies a gene to earn royalties on any test or therapy created with that gene. A British hospital that tested a patient for cystic fibrosis was asked to pay royalties because a private company held the patent on the gene.[20] Some laboratories are giving up a useful hormone test to determine whether a fetus has Down's syndrome because the royalty fees exceed Medicaid reimbursement.[21] A patent monopoly on cord blood storage would hamper the development of community cord blood banks, leaving patients who do not have the money to store their infant's blood without a remedy if their child develops a disorder requiring a cord blood transplantation. The real costs in such cases are borne by patients denied appropriate treatment....

But as biomedical research becomes more closely tied to commercial goals, the encroachment of the market is triggering a growing sense of disillusionment and mistrust. For the encroachment of commercial practices on the human body is increasingly challenging individual and cultural values, encouraging exploitation through the collection and use of tissue, and turning tissue (and potentially people) into marketable products.

## NOTES FOR READING EIGHT

1 David Cox, Stanford University, personal communication.

2 Heather Kirby, "Something Nasty in the Night Cream," *The Times* (London), 3 April 1992.

3 See, for example, Andrew Kimbrell, *The Human Body Shop: The Engineering and Marketing of Life* (San Francisco: Harper San Francisco, 1993); Sheldon Krimsky, *Biotechnics and Society* (New York: Praeger, 1991); and Paul Rabinow, *Making PCR* (Chicago: University of Chicago Press, 1996).

4 Diamond v. Chakabarty, 447 U.S. 303 (1980). Initially, researchers assumed that genes were not patentable since patent law covers "inventions" and prohibits patenting the "products of nature."

5 Quoted in John Vidal and Hohn Carvel, "Lambs to the Gene Market," *The Guardian* (London), 12 November 1994.

6 Moore v. Regents of the University of California, p. 495.

7 The distribution of genes across populations can also help answer intriguing questions about human origins and patterns of migration. L. L. Cavalli-Sforza, A. C. Wilson, C. R. Cantor et al., "Survey of Human Genetic Diversity: A Vanishing Opportunity for the Human Genome Project," *Genomics* 11 (1991): 490-91.

8 Zef Productions, Ltd., "The Gene Hunters," documentary film, aired by British Broadcasting, Channel 4, 1995.

9 World Council of Indigenous People, "Resolution on the HGDP," *Native Net Archive Page* http://broc09.uthsca.edu/natnet/archive/nl/hgdp.html.

10 "The Human Body Parts Trade," *World Press Review* 1, no. 4 (1994): 38.

11 Charles M. Sennott, "New Cold War: Spies Target Corporation," *Boston Globe*, 19 January 1997.

12 CBS Evening News, 21 May 1996.

13 Catherine Tastemain, "Oversight for Tissue Transplants," *Nature-Medicine* 1, no. 5 (1995): 397.

14 Karen Brandon, "Emerging Fertility Scandal Has Californians Rapt," *Chicago Tribune*, 24 March 1996.

15 Global 2000, Communiqué, 1997.

16 Barbara Bernier, "Class, Race and Poverty: Medical Technologies and Socio-Political Choices," *Harvard BlackLetter* 11 (1994): 115.

17 Sheldon Krimsky et al., "Financial Interests of Authors on Scientific Journals," *Science and Energy Ethics* 2 (1996): 395-410.

18 David Blumenthal et al., "Participation of Life Science Faculty in Research Relations with Industry," *NEJM* 335 (1996): 1734-39; and Sheldon Krimsky et al., "Financial Interests."

19 Tim Friend, "Gene Trailblazers Past Warp," *USA Today*, 24 June 1997.

20 U.K. Clinical Molecular Genetics Society, Statement, "Opposing Gene Patenting," 1996.

21 Kurt Eichemwald, "Push for Royalties Threatens Use of Down's Syndrome Test," *New York Times*, 23 May 1997.

READING

**9**

# OWNING TISSUE: THE POINT

### Justice Edward Panelli

*Justice Edward Panelli authored the majority opinion for the Supreme Court of California in* Moore v. The Regents of the University of California, et al. *(1990). The majority affirmed in part and reversed in part, an earlier ruling by the Court of Appeal.*

■ **POINTS TO CONSIDER**

1. Summarize the complaint of John Moore.

2. Who owns John Moore's cells, according to the majority?

3. Define "conversion." How does Moore attempt to characterize the invasion of his rights as a conversion?

4. Identify the court's ruling on Moore's conversion claim. What overriding "policy consideration" motivated this ruling?

5. Discuss the opinion on Dr. David Golde's responsibility. Do you agree with the court?

Excerpted from *John Moore v. The Regents of the University of California, et al.*, No. S006987, Supreme Court of California, 51 Cal. 3d 120; 793 P. 2d 479; 1990.

*The important policy consideration is that we not threaten with disabling civil liability innocent parties who are engaged in socially useful activities, such as researchers who have no reason to believe that their use of a particular cell sample is, or may be, against a donor's wishes.*

[The Plaintiff] Moore first visited the UCLA Medical Center on October 5, 1976, shortly after he learned that he had hairy cell leukemia. After hospitalizing Moore and "withdrawing extensive amounts of blood, bone marrow aspirate, and other bodily substances," [Dr. David] Golde confirmed [a hairy cell leukemia] diagnosis. At this time all defendants, including Golde, were aware that "certain blood products and blood components were of great value in a number of commercial and scientific efforts" and that access to a patient whose blood contained these substances would provide "competitive, commercial, and scientific advantages."

## DOCTOR'S ORDERS

On October 8, 1976, Golde recommended that Moore's spleen be removed. Golde informed Moore "that he had reason to fear for his life, and that the proposed splenectomy operation...was necessary to slow down the progress of his disease." Based upon Golde's representations, Moore signed a written consent form authorizing the splenectomy.

Before the operation, Golde and [UCLA Researcher Shirley G.] Quan "formed the intent and made arrangements to obtain portions of [Moore's] spleen following its removal" and to take them to a separate research unit. Golde gave written instructions to this effect on October 18 and 19, 1976. These research activities "were not intended to have...any relation to [Moore's] medical...care." However, neither Golde nor Quan informed Moore of their plans to conduct this research or requested his permission. Surgeons at the UCLA Medical Center, whom the complaint does not name as defendants, removed Moore's spleen on October 20, 1976.

Moore returned to the UCLA Medical Center several times between November 1976 and September 1983. He did so at Golde's direction and based upon representations "that such visits were necessary and required for his health and well-being, and based upon the trust inherent in and by virtue of the physician-patient relationship..." On each of these visits Golde withdrew additional samples of "blood, blood serum, skin, bone marrow aspirate, and sperm." On each occasion Moore travelled to the UCLA Medical Center from his home in Seattle because he had been told that the procedures were to be performed only there and only under Golde's direction.

## PATENTED CELLS

Sometime before August 1979, Golde established a cell line from Moore's T-lymphocytes. On January 30, 1981, the [University of California] Regents applied for a patent on the cell line, listing Golde and Quan as inventors. "By virtue of an established policy..., [the] Regents, Golde, and Quan would share in any royalties or profits...arising out of [the] patent." The patent issued on March 20, 1984, naming Golde and Quan as the inventors of the cell line and the Regents as the assignee of the patent. (U.S. Patent No. 4,438,032 [Mar. 20, 1984].)

The Regents' patent also covers various methods for using the cell line to produce lymphokines. Moore admits in his complaint that "the true clinical potential of each of the lymphokines...[is] difficult to predict, [but]...competing commercial firms in these relevant fields have published reports in biotechnology industry periodicals predicting a potential market of approximately 3.01 billion dollars by the year 1990 for a whole range of [such lymphokines]...."

With the Regents' assistance, Golde negotiated agreements for commercial development of the cell line and products to be derived from it. Under an agreement with Genetics Institute, Golde "became a 'paid consultant' and acquired the rights to 75,000 shares of common stock." Genetics Institute also agreed to pay Golde and the Regents "at least $330,000 over three years, including a *pro rata* share of [Golde's] salary and fringe benefits, in exchange for...exclusive access to the materials and research performed" on the cell line and products derived from it. On June 4, 1982, Sandoz "was added to the agreement," and compensation payable to Golde and the Regents was increased by $110,000. "Throughout this period,...Quan spent as much as 70 [percent] of her time working for [the] Regents on research" related to the cell line.

## LACK OF INFORMED CONSENT

Moore repeatedly alleges that Golde failed to disclose the extent of his research and economic interests in Moore's cells before obtaining consent to the medical procedures by which the cells were extracted. These allegations, in our view, state a cause of action against Golde for invading a legally protected interest of his patient. Even if the splenectomy had a therapeutic purpose, it does not follow that Golde had no duty to disclose his additional research and economic interests. The existence of a motivation for a medical procedure unrelated to the patient's health is a potential conflict of interest and a fact material to the patient's decision.

## CONVERSION

Moore also attempts to characterize the invasion of his rights as a "conversion" — a tort that protects against interference with possessory and ownership interests in personal property. He theorizes that he continued to own his cells following their removal from his body, at least for the purpose of directing their use, and that he never consented to their use in potentially lucrative medical research. Thus, to complete Moore's argument, defendants' unauthorized use of his cells constitutes a conversion. As a result of the alleged conversion, Moore claims a proprietary interest in each of the products that any of the defendants might ever create from his cells or the patented cell line.

No court, however, has ever in a reported decision imposed conversion liability for the use of human cells in medical research. While that fact does not end our inquiry, it raises a flag of caution. In effect, what Moore is asking us to do is to impose a tort duty on scientists to investigate the consensual pedigree of each human cell sample used in research. To impose such a duty, which would affect medical research of importance to all of society, implicates policy concerns far removed from the traditional, two-party ownership disputes in which the law of conversion arose. Invoking a tort theory originally used to determine whether the loser or the finder of a horse had the better title, Moore claims ownership of the results of socially important medical research, including the genetic code for chemicals that regulate the functions of every human being's immune system.

## OWNERSHIP

Since Moore clearly did not expect to retain possession of his cells following their removal, to sue for their conversion he must have retained an ownership interest in them. But there are several reasons to doubt that he did retain any such interest. First, no reported judicial decision supports Moore's claim, either directly or by close analogy. Second, California statutory law drastically limits any continuing interest of a patient in excised cells. Third, the subject matters of the Regents' patent — the patented cell line and the products derived from it — cannot be Moore's property.

A consideration that makes Moore's claim of ownership problematic is California statutory law, which drastically limits a patient's control over excised cells. Pursuant to Health and Safety Code section 7054.4, "notwithstanding any other provision of law, recognizable anatomical parts, human tissues, anatomical human remains, or infectious waste following conclusion of scientific use shall be disposed of by interment, incineration, or any other method determined by the state department [of health services] to protect the public health and safety." By restricting how excised cells may be used and requiring their eventual destruction, the statute eliminates so many of the rights ordinarily attached to property that one cannot simply assume that what is left amounts to "property" or "ownership" for purposes of conversion law.

## PROPERTY AND PATENTS

The subject matter of the Regents' patent — the patented cell line and the products derived from it — cannot be Moore's property. This is because the patented cell line is both factually and legally distinct from the cells taken from Moore's body. Federal law permits the patenting of organisms that represent the product of "human ingenuity," but not naturally occurring organisms (*Diamond* v. *Chakrabarty* (1980) 447 U.S. 303). It is this *inventive effort* that patent law rewards, not the discovery of naturally occurring raw materials. Thus, Moore's allegations that he owns the cell line and the products derived from it are inconsistent with the patent, which constitutes an authoritative determination that the cell line is the product of invention. Since such allegations are nothing more than arguments or conclusions of law, they of course do not bind us.

## CONVERSION LIABILITY

There are three reasons why it is inappropriate to impose liability for conversion based upon the allegations of Moore's complaint. First, a fair balancing of the relevant policy considerations counsels against extending the tort. Second, problems in this area are better suited to legislative resolution. Third, the tort of conversion is not necessary to protect patients' rights. For these reasons, we conclude that the use of excised human cells in medical research does not amount to a conversion.

Of the relevant policy considerations, two are of overriding importance. The first is protection of a competent patient's right to make autonomous medical decisions. That right is grounded in well-recognized and long-standing principles of fiduciary duty and informed consent. This policy weighs in favor of providing a remedy to patients when physicians act with undisclosed motives that may affect their professional judgment. The second important policy consideration is that we not threaten with disabling civil liability innocent parties who are engaged in socially useful activities, such as researchers who have no reason to believe that their use of a particular cell sample is, or may be, against a donor's wishes.

In deciding whether to create new tort duties we have in the past considered the impact that expanded liability would have on activities that are important to society, such as research. For example, in *Brown* v. *Superior Court, supra,* 44 Cal.3d 1049, the fear that strict product liability would frustrate pharmaceutical research led us to hold that a drug manufacturer's liability should not be measured by those standards. We wrote that, "if drug manufacturers were subject to strict liability, they might be reluctant to undertake research programs to develop some pharmaceuticals that would prove beneficial or to distribute others that are available to be marketed, because of the fear of large adverse monetary judgments." (*Id.,* at p. 1063.)

## REALM OF LEGISLATURE

If the scientific users of human cells are to be held liable for failing to investigate the consensual pedigree of their raw materials, we believe the Legislature should make that decision. Complex policy choices affecting all society are involved, and "legislatures, in making such policy decisions, have the ability to gather empirical evidence, solicit the advice of experts, and hold hearings at which all interested parties present evidence and express their views..." (*Foley* v. *Interactive Data Corp., supra,* 47 Cal.3d at p. 694, fn. 31.) Legislative competence to act in this area is demonstrated by the existing statutes governing the use and disposition of human biological materials.

## CONSENT, NOT CONVERSION

Finally, there is no pressing need to impose a judicially created rule of strict liability, since enforcement of physicians' disclosure obligations will protect patients against the very type of harm with which Moore was threatened. So long as a physician discloses research and economic interests that may affect his judgment, the patient is protected from conflicts of interest. Aware of any conflicts, the patient can make an informed decision to consent to treatment, or to withhold consent and look elsewhere for medical assistance. As already discussed, enforcement of physicians' disclosure obligations protects patients directly, without hindering the socially useful activities of innocent researchers.

For these reasons, we hold that the allegations of Moore's third amended complaint state a cause of action for breach of fiduciary duty or lack of informed consent, but not conversion.

READING

**10**

# OWNING TISSUE: THE COUNTERPOINT

## Justice Stanley Mosk

*Justice Stanley Mosk has served on the California Supreme Court since 1964. He authored the dissent in* Moore v. The Regents, *affirming an earlier decision of the Court of Appeal to direct the trial court to overrule the respondent's demurrers.*

### ■ POINTS TO CONSIDER

1. How does Mosk evaluate John Moore's claims of ownership of his cells? According to Mosk, how does the Mo cell patent affect Moore's claims?

2. Evaluate the Court of Appeal's statement "Defendants' position that plaintiff cannot own his tissue, but that they can, is fraught with irony."

3. Name and discuss the two policy considerations which override, in Mosk's dissent, the majority's concern regarding socially valuable research.

4. According to Mosk, what is problematic about the patient only retaining the right to refuse consent?

---

Excerpted from *John Moore v. The Regents of the University of California, et al.,* No. S006987, Supreme Court of California, 51 Cal. 3d 120; 793 P. 2d 479; 1990.

*Our society acknowledges a profound ethical impera-tive to respect the human body as the physical and temporal expression of the unique human persona.*

Contrary to the principal holding of the Court of Appeal, the majority conclude that the complaint does not — in fact cannot — state a cause of action for conversion. I disagree with this con-clusion for all the reasons stated by the Court of Appeal, and for additional reasons that I shall explain.

## OWNERSHIP INTEREST

The majority first take the position that Moore has no cause of action for conversion under existing law because he retained no "ownership interest" in his cells after they were removed from his body.

The majority's first reason is that "no reported judicial decision supports Moore's claim, either directly or by close analogy." Neither, however, is there any reported decision rejecting such a claim. The issue is as new as its source — the recent explosive growth in the commercialization of biotechnology.

I need not review the many instances in which this court has broken fresh ground by announcing new rules of tort law: time and again when a new rule was needed we did not stay our hand merely because the matter was one of first impression.

The majority's second reason for doubting that Moore retained an ownership interest in his cells after their excision is that "California statutory law...drastically limits a patient's control over excised cells." For this proposition the majority rely on Health and Safety Code section 7054.4.

By its terms, section 7054.4 permits only "scientific use" of excised body parts and tissue before they must be destroyed. It would stretch the English language beyond recognition, however, to say that commercial exploitation of the kind and degree alleged here is also a usual and ordinary meaning of the phrase "scientific use."

Secondly, even if section 7054.4 does permit defendants' com-mercial exploitation of Moore's tissue under the guise of "scientif-ic use," it does not follow that — as the majority conclude — the statute "eliminates so many of the rights ordinarily attached to

71

property" that what remains does not amount to "property" or "ownership" for purposes of the law of conversion.

## IRONY

At the time of its excision [Moore] at least had *the right to do with his own tissue whatever the defendants did with it:* i.e., he could have contracted with researchers and pharmaceutical companies to develop and exploit the vast commercial potential of his tissue and its products. Defendants certainly believe that *their* right to do the foregoing is not barred by section 7054.4 and is a significant property right, as they have demonstrated by their deliberate concealment from Moore of the true value of his tissue, their efforts to obtain a patent on the Mo cell line, their contractual agreements to exploit this material, their exclusion of Moore from any participation in the profits, and their vigorous defense of this lawsuit. The Court of Appeal summed up the point by observing that "Defendants' position that plaintiff cannot own his tissue, but that they can, is fraught with irony." It is also legally untenable. As noted above, the majority cite no case holding that an individual's right to develop and exploit the commercial potential of his own tissue is *not* a right of sufficient worth or dignity to be deemed a protectible property interest. In the absence of such authority — or of legislation to the same effect — the right falls within the traditionally broad concept of property in our law.

## FAIRNESS, EQUITY AND COMPENSATION

The majority assert in effect that Moore cannot have an ownership interest in the Mo cell line because defendants patented it. To be sure, the patent granted defendants the exclusive right to make, use, or sell the invention for a period of 17 years. (35 U.S.C. § 154.) But Moore does not assert any such right for himself. Rather, he seeks to show that he is entitled, in fairness and equity, to some share in the profits that defendants have made and will make from their commercial exploitation of the Mo cell line. I do not question that the cell line is primarily the product of defendants' inventive effort. Yet likewise no one can question Moore's crucial contribution to the invention — an invention named, ironically, after him: but for the cells of Moore's body taken by defendants, *there would have been no Mo cell line.*

Nevertheless the majority conclude that the patent somehow cut off all Moore's rights — past, present, and future — to share in the proceeds of defendants' commercial exploitation of the cell line derived from his own body tissue. The majority cite no authority for this unfair result, and I cannot believe it is compelled by the general law of patents: a patent is not a license to defraud.

The law of patents would not be a bar to Moore's assertion of an ownership interest in his cells and their products sufficient to warrant his sharing in the proceeds of their commercial exploitation.

## POLICY CONSIDERATION

Having concluded — mistakenly, in my view — that Moore has no cause of action for conversion under existing law, the majority next consider whether to "extend" the conversion cause of action to this context. Again the majority find reasons not to do so, and again I respectfully disagree with each.

The majority focus on policy consideration, i.e., their concern "that we not threaten with disabling civil liability innocent parties who are engaged in socially useful activities, such as researchers who have no reason to believe that their use of a particular cell sample is, or may be, against a donor's wishes." As will appear, in my view this concern is both overstated and outweighed by contrary considerations.

In any event, in my view whatever merit the majority's single policy consideration may have is outweighed by two contrary considerations, i.e., policies that are promoted by recognizing that every individual has a legally protectible property interest in his own body and its products. First, our society acknowledges a profound ethical imperative to respect the human body as the physical and temporal expression of the unique human persona. One manifestation of that respect is our prohibition against direct abuse of the body by torture or other forms of cruel or unusual punishment. Another is our prohibition against indirect abuse of the body by its economic exploitation for the sole benefit of another person. The most abhorrent form of such exploitation, of course, was the institution of slavery. Lesser forms, such as indentured servitude or even debtor's prison, have also disappeared. Yet their specter haunts the laboratories and boardrooms of today's biotechnological research-industrial complex. It arises wherever scientists or industrialists claim, as defendants claim here, the right to appropriate and exploit a patient's tissue for their sole economic benefit — the right, in other words, to freely mine or harvest valuable physical properties of the patient's body.

73

## POWER AND PARITY

A second policy consideration adds notions of equity to those of ethics. Our society values fundamental fairness in dealings between its members, and condemns the unjust enrichment of any member at the expense of another. This is particularly true when, as here, the parties are not in equal bargaining positions. We are repeatedly told that the commercial products of the biotechnological revolution "hold the promise of tremendous profit." In the case at bar, for example, the complainant alleges that the market for the kinds of proteins produced by the Mo cell line was predicted to exceed three billion dollars by 1990. These profits are currently shared exclusively between the biotechnology industry and the universities that support that industry. The profits are shared in a wide variety of ways, including "direct entrepreneurial ties to genetic-engineering firms" and "an equity interest in fledgling biotechnology firms" (Howard, *supra*, 44 Food Drug Cosm. L.J. at p. 338). Thus the complainant alleges that because of his development of the Mo cell line defendant Golde became a paid consultant of defendant Genetics Institute and acquired the rights to 75,000 shares of that firm's stock at a cost of one cent each; that Genetics Institute further contracted to pay Golde and the Regents at least $330,000 over three years, including a *pro rata* share of Golde's salary and fringe benefits; and that defendant Sandoz Pharmaceuticals Corporation subsequently contracted to increase that compensation by a further $110,000.

## CRITICAL CONTRIBUTION

There is, however, a third party to the biotechnology enterprise — the patient who is the source of the blood or tissue from which all these profits are derived. While he may be a silent partner, his contribution to the venture is absolutely crucial: as pointed out above, but for the cells of Moore's body taken by defendants there would have been no Mo cell line at all. Yet defendants deny that Moore is entitled to any share whatever in the proceeds of this cell line. This is both inequitable and immoral. As Dr. Thomas H. Murray, a respected professor of ethics and public policy, testified before Congress, "the person [who furnishes the tissue] should be justly compensated...If biotechnologists fail to make provision for a just sharing of profits with the person whose gift made it possible, the public's sense of justice will be offended and no one will be the winner."

## LEGISLATURE

The majority's second reason for declining to extend the conversion cause of action to the present context is that "the Legislature should make that decision." I do not doubt that the Legislature is competent to act on this topic. The fact that the Legislature may intervene if and when it chooses, however, does not in the meanwhile relieve the courts of their duty of enforcing — or if need be, fashioning — an effective judicial remedy for the wrong here alleged.

The majority hold that a physician who intends to treat a patient in whom he has either a research interest or an economic interest is under a fiduciary duty to disclose such interest to the patient before treatment, that his failure to do so may give rise to a nondisclosure cause of action, and that the complaint herein states such a cause of action at least against defendant Golde. I agree with that holding as far as it goes.

I disagree, however, with the majority's further conclusion that in the present context a nondisclosure cause of action is an adequate — in fact, a superior — substitute for a conversion cause of action. In my view the non disclosure cause of action falls short.

The reason why the nondisclosure cause of action is inadequate for the task that the majority assign to it is that it fails to solve half the problem before us: it gives the patient only the right to *refuse* consent, i.e., the right to prohibit the commercialization of his tissue; it does not give him the right to *grant* consent to that commercialization on the condition that he share in its proceeds.

## NO COMPENSATION

Reversing the words of the old song, the nondisclosure cause of action thus accentuates the negative and eliminates the positive: the patient can say *no,* but he cannot say *yes* and expect to share in the proceeds of his contribution. Yet as explained above, there are sound reasons of ethics and equity to recognize the patient's right to participate in such benefits. The nondisclosure cause of action does not protect that right; to that extent, it is therefore not an adequate substitute for the conversion remedy, which does protect the right.

I would affirm the decision of the Court of Appeal to direct the trial court to overrule the demurrers to the cause of action for conversion.

75

# RECOGNIZING AUTHOR'S POINT OF VIEW

*This activity may be used as an individualized study guide for students in libraries and resource centers or as a discussion catalyst in small group and classroom discussions.*

## Source Descriptions

a. Essentially an article that related factual information

b. Essentially an article that expresses editorial points of view

c. Both of the above

d. Neither of the above

## Readings in Chapter Two:

1.

_____ Reading Eight

"Homo Economicus: Considerations in the Commercialization of Body Tissue," by Dorothy Nelson and Lori Andrews

_____ Reading Nine

"Owning Tissue: The Point," by Justice Edward Panelli

_____ Reading Ten

"Owning Tissue: The Counterpoint," by Justice Stanley Mosk

76

2. Summarize the author's point of view in one to three sentences for each of the readings in Chapter Two.

3. After careful consideration, pick out one reading that you think is the most reliable source. Be prepared to explain the reasons for your choice in a general class discussion.

4. Explain the point and counterpoint. Which do you agree with? Why?

## CHAPTER 3

# FRANKENFOOD OR FUTURE OF FARMING? AG BIOTECH

# PLANT BIOTECHNOLOGY: FARMING OF THE FUTURE

## Monsanto

*Monsanto is a Saint Louis-based life sciences company specializing in agricultural products, pharmaceuticals and food ingredients.*

■ **POINTS TO CONSIDER**

1. Describe the relationship between traditional plant breeding and biotechnology. What is the difference, according to Monsanto?

2. What is B.t. and what is Monsanto doing with B.t.?

3. How does Monsanto aim to protect crops from disease?

4. Discuss the reasoning behind herbicide-tolerant crops.

Excerpted from "Increasing the World's Food Supply through Plant Biotechnology," **Biobrochure**/Page 4, St. Louis: Monsanto Corporation, 1998. Available at www. monsanto.com/, reprinted by permission.

**Crop improvements can help provide an abundant, healthful food supply and protect our environment for future generations.**

For centuries, farmers have made improvements in crop plants through selective breeding and hybridization — the controlled pollination of plants. Plant biotechnology is an extension of this traditional plant breeding with one very important difference — plant biotechnology allows for the transfer of a greater variety of genetic information in a more precise, controlled manner.

Unlike traditional plant breeding, which involves the crossing of hundreds of genes, plant biotechnology allows for the transfer of only one or a few desirable genes. This more precise science allows plant breeders to develop crops with specific beneficial traits and without undesirable traits, such as those that would reduce crop yields.

Many of these beneficial traits in new plant varieties fight plant pests — insects, disease and weeds — that can be devastating to crops. Others provide quality improvements, such as tastier fruits and vegetables; processing advantages, such as tomatoes with higher solids content; and nutrition enhancements, such as oil seeds that produce oils with lower saturated fat content. Crop improvements like these can help provide an abundant, healthful food supply and protect our environment for future generations.

## INSECT PROTECTION

Anyone who has planted a backyard garden is familiar with the potential devastation caused by insect pests. Farmers also face these problems on a *much larger* scale. For example, the Colorado potato beetle can strip a field of potato plants in less than a week. To fight this pest, farmers in many parts of the country must spray insecticides up to five times per season.

*Bacillus thuringiensis* (B.t.) — a naturally occurring bacterium present in soil — is known for its ability to control insect pests. Different strains of B.t. control different pests. First discovered in 1902, B.t. has been used by gardeners for decades as a biological insecticide spray. B.t. produces a protein that disrupts the digestive system of targeted insects, while remaining harmless to other insects, people, birds and other animals.

Now through biotechnology, researchers are introducing the

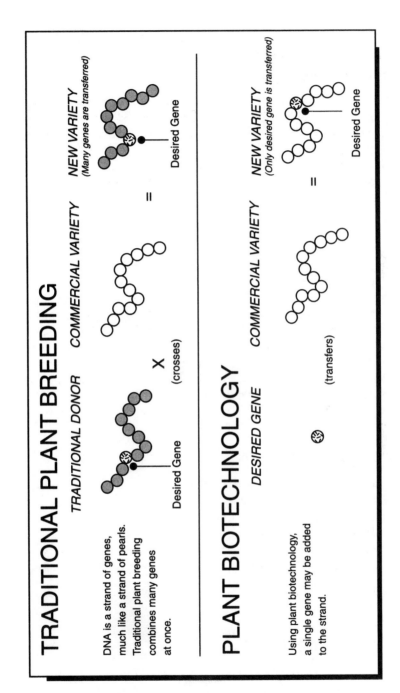

# TRADITIONAL PLANT BREEDING

**TRADITIONAL DONOR**

Desired Gene

X
(crosses)

**COMMERCIAL VARIETY**

=

**NEW VARIETY**
*(Many genes are transferred)*

Desired Gene

DNA is a strand of genes,
much like a strand of pearls.
Traditional plant breeding
combines many genes
at once.

# PLANT BIOTECHNOLOGY

**DESIRED GENE**

(transfers)

**COMMERCIAL VARIETY**

=

**NEW VARIETY**
*(Only desired gene is transferred)*

Desired Gene

Using plant biotechnology,
a single gene may be added
to the strand.

Reprinted by permission, **Monsanto.**

81

B.t. gene into plants, which allows the plants to protect themselves from certain insect pests. For example, Monsanto's NewLeaf® potato plants are protected from the Colorado potato beetle. Monsanto also has developed cotton with the Bollgard® gene that protects the crop from the tobacco budworm, cotton bollworm and pink bollworm, and YieldGard® corn, which is protected from the European corn borer.

Insect-protected crops offer agricultural and environmental benefits. For example, when farmers decrease chemical insecticide use, beneficial insects can survive to help control other harmful insects. There also is less potential exposure of farmers and groundwater to chemical insecticides and greater compatibility with Integrated Pest Management — a sustainable, ecological approach to pest control drawing on many farming methods, including biological, chemical and mechanical methods. In addition, insect-protected crops, such as NewLeaf potato and cotton with the Bollgard gene, offer farmers season-long, effective control and ease of use. They also reduce the time, effort and resources spent, requiring fewer trips across the field, which helps preserve topsoil.

## DISEASE PROTECTION

Plant disease, including fungal and viral diseases, can devastate the yield and quality of crop production. To minimize the economic loss resulting from plant disease, farmers often must plant more acreage than they expect to harvest. This extra acreage increases farmers' planting, fuel, water and fertilizer expenses, which must be passed on to the consumer.

In addition, many farmers fight viral plant disease by controlling insect pests, such as aphids, that carry the disease. Thus, chemical insecticide use contributes to the mounting costs and resources necessary to offset the effects of plant disease.

Not all farmers can afford the costs of these traditional methods of disease control. The expense of chemical insecticides is prohibitive in many parts of the world, such as parts of Africa, where, for example, the feathery mottle virus often destroys two-thirds of farmers' sweet potato harvests.

Biotechnology makes possible the development of crops protected from certain types of plant viruses. By introducing a small part of the DNA from a virus into the genetic makeup of a plant, researchers have developed crops that have built-in immunity to targeted diseases.

Disease-protected crops offer agricultural, economic and environmental benefits to farmers. Farmers will be able to control insects that carry viral disease, and they will be able to protect their crop yields. Farmers may be able to produce a higher yield on the same amount of acres, while reducing resources used, such as the expense of labor, fuel, pesticides, seed and equipment. These savings may enable farmers to plant additional acres; or the increased yield per acre may enable them to plant fewer acres, resulting in increased soil conservation.

Using biotechnology, today's researchers are working to protect alfalfa, canola, cantaloupe, corn, cucumbers, grapes, potatoes, soybeans, squash and tomatoes from viral disease as well as peppers and tomatoes from fungal disease.

## WEED CONTROL

Farmers have battled weeds since the beginning of farming. Weeds not only compete with crops for water, nutrients, sunlight and space, but also harbor insect and disease pests; clog irrigation and drainage systems; undermine crop quality; and deposit weed seeds into crop harvests.

Farmers can fight weeds with tillage, herbicides or, typically, a combination of these techniques. Unfortunately, tillage leaves valuable topsoil exposed to wind and water erosion, a serious long-term consequence for the environment. For this reason, more and more farmers prefer reduced or no-till methods of farming.

Herbicide-tolerant crops offer farmers a vital tool in fighting weeds and are compatible with no-till methods, which help preserve topsoil. Herbicide-tolerant crops give farmers the flexibility to apply herbicides only when needed, to control total input of herbicides and to use herbicides with preferred environmental characteristics.

Monsanto researchers have developed herbicide-tolerant crops, such as canola, corn, cotton and soybean, that can tolerate Roundup® herbicide, a non-selective product with favorable environmental characteristics that have been widely recognized. Roundup effectively controls a broad range of grasses and broadleaf weeds by inhibiting EPSP synthase, an enzyme essential to plants' growth. In other words, Roundup® inhibits growth by establishing a roadblock in plants' metabolic pathways. The gene inserted into these herbicide-tolerant crops — known as Roundup Ready® crops — increases the amount of EPSP synthase protein in the plants, providing a detour around the roadblock. This detour makes it possible for Roundup Ready crops to thrive even after Roundup is used over the top of the growing crop to control weeds.

## DESIRABLE TRAITS

Roundup's desirable environmental traits include tightly binding to soil particles and breaking down in the soil over time into naturally occurring components, such as carbon dioxide. Also, it is highly unlikely to reach ground water. First registered and introduced in the United States in 1974, glyphosate, the active ingredient in Roundup, now is registered in more than 100 countries worldwide.

Traditionally, farmers have applied residual herbicides that stayed in the soil before and after the crops emerged for weed control. With the ability to apply Roundup on an "as needed" basis over the top of crops, farmers can use Roundup only when necessary. As a result, they may be able to reduce the number and amount of herbicide applications during the growing season.

## OTHER CROP IMPROVEMENTS

By introducing a gene or genes into a crop plant, many other advantageous features may be possible. Examples include:

- A genetic trait that controls the ripening of tomatoes, peppers and tropical fruits. This trait allows time to ship crops long distances and results in tastier foods far from crops' native regions.

- Potatoes and tomatoes developed with higher solids content. This trait offers decreased processing costs because less energy is needed to extract water when producing potato and tomato products. The higher solids content of potatoes holds the potential to bring consumers lower fat French fries. Because oil replaces water during the frying process, potatoes with higher solids content (and less water) absorb less oil....

# PLANT BIOTECHNOLOGY: ENVIRONMENTAL QUESITONS

## Brian Halweil

*Brian Halweil is a staff researcher at the WorldWatch Institute. The WorldWatch Institute is a nonprofit research organization which monitors and evaluates changes in climate, forest cover, population, food production, biological diversity and other key trends. Its aim is to identify and analyze the most effective means for achieving sustainable society. Contact WorldWatch at 1776 Massachusetts Avenue, NW, Washington, D.C. 20036; (202) 452-1999, worldwatch@worldwatch.org.*

### ■ POINTS TO CONSIDER

1. Describe the current pesticide paradigm, according to Halweil.

2. Discuss the author's view on the ecological consequences of HRCs and insecticidal transgenic crops.

3. Define genetic pollution.

4. Explain the author's concern about patenting genes. What effect might this have on agriculture in the First and Third Worlds?

Excerpted from Kathryn Collmer, "From Hand to Mouth," **Sojourners,** June 1993. Reprinted with permission from **Sojourners,** 2401 15th Street NW, Washington, D.C. 20009; (202) 328-8842/(800) 714-7474.

*If the industry continues to follow its current trajectory, then biotech's likely contribution will be marginal at best and at worst, given the additional dimensions of ecological and social unpredictability – who knows?*

...In the early 1980s, several research teams — including one at Monsanto, then a multinational pesticide company — succeeded in splicing a bacterium gene into a petunia. The first "transgenic" plant was born.

## QUANTUM LEAP

Such plants represented a quantum leap in crop breeding: the fact that a plant could not interbreed with a bacterium was no longer an obstacle to using the microbe's genes in crop design. Theoretically, at least, the world's entire store of genetic wealth became available to plant breeders, and the biotech labs were quick to test the new possibilities. Among the early creations was a tomato armed with a flounder gene to enhance frost resistance and with a rebuilt tomato gene to retard spoilage. A variety of the oilseed crop known as rape or canola was outfitted with a gene from the California Bay tree to alter the composition of its oil. A potato was endowed with bacterial resistance from a chicken gene.

Transgenic crops are no longer just a laboratory phenomenon. Since 1986, 25,000 transgenic field trials have been conducted worldwide — a full 10,000 of these just in the last two years. More than 60 different crops — ranging from corn to strawberries, from apples to potatoes — have been engineered. From two million hectares in 1996, the global area planted in transgenics jumped to 27.8 million hectares in 1998. That's nearly a fifteenfold increase in just two years....

Two types of crops — the insecticidal and the herbicide-resistant varieties — are biotech's first large-scale commercial ventures. They provide the first real opportunity to test the industry's claims to be engineering a new agricultural paradigm.

## THE BUGS

The only insecticidal transgenics currently in commercial use are "B.t. crops." Grown on nearly eight million hectares worldwide in 1998, these plants have been equipped with a gene from

## GLOBAL TRANSGENIC AREA, 1996-98

| Country | 1996 | 1997 | 1998 | Share of global area, 1998 |
|---|---|---|---|---|
| | *(million hectares)* | | | *(percent)* |
| United States | 1.5 | 8.1 | 20.5 | 74 |
| Argentina | 0.1 | 1.4 | 4.3 | 15 |
| Canada | 0.1 | 1.3 | 2.8 | 10 |
| Australia | <0.1 | 0.1 | 0.1 | 1 |
| Mexico | <0.1 | <0.1 | 0.1 | 1 |
| Spain | – | – | <0.1 | <1 |
| France | – | – | <0.1 | <1 |
| South Africa | – | – | <0.1 | <1 |
| TOTAL | 1.7 | 11.0 | 27.8 | 100 |

Note: China is not included because of uncertainty over the extent of area planted, but a rough estimate for 1998 is one million hectares.

SOURCE: Clive James, *Global Review of Commercialized Transgenic Crops: 1998* (Ithaca, NY: International Service for the Acquisition of Agri-biotech Applications, 1998).

the soil organism *Bacillus thuringiensis* (B.t.), which produces a substance that is deadly to certain insects.

The idea behind B.t. crops is to free conventional agriculture from the highly toxic synthetic pesticides that have defined pest control since World War II. [CEO Robert] Shapiro, for instance, speaks of Monsanto's B.t. cotton as a way of substituting "information encoded in a gene in a cotton plant for airplanes flying over cotton fields and spraying toxic chemicals on them." (As with other high technologies, the substitution of information for stuff is a fundamental doctrine of biotech.) At least in the short term, B.t. varieties have allowed farmers to cut their spraying of insecticide-intensive crops, like cotton and potato. In 1998, for instance, the typical B.t. cotton grower in Mississippi sprayed only once for tobacco budworm and cotton bollworm — the insects targeted by B.t. — while non-B.t. growers averaged five sprayings.

Farmers are buying into this approach in a big way. B.t. crops have had some of the highest adoption rates that the seed industry has ever seen for new varieties. In the United States, just a few years after commercialization, nearly 25 percent of the corn crop and 20 percent of the cotton crop is B.t. In some counties in the southeastern states, the adoption rate of B.t. cotton has reached 70 percent. The big draw for farmers is a lowering of production costs from reduced insecticide spraying, although the savings is partly offset by the more expensive seed. Some farmers also report that B.t. crops are doing a better job of pest control than conventional spraying, although the crops must still be sprayed for pests that are unaffected by B.t. (B.t. is toxic primarily to members of the *Lepidoptera*, the butterfly and moth family, and the *Coleoptera*, the beetle family.)...

The B.t. transgenics basically just replace an insecticide that is sprayed on the crop with one that is packaged inside it. The technique may be more sophisticated but the strategy remains the same: aim the chemical at the pest. Some entomologists are predicting that, without comprehensive strategies to prevent it, pest resistance to B.t. could appear in the field within three to five years of widespread use, rendering the crops ineffective. Widespread resistance to B.t. would affect more than the transgenic crops, since B.t. is also commonly used in conventional spraying. Farmers could find one of their most environmentally benign pesticides beginning to slip away....

## THE WEEDS

The global transgenic harvest is currently dominated, not by B.t. crops, but by herbicide-resistant crops (HRCs), which occupy 20 million hectares worldwide. HRCs are sold as part of a "technology package" comprised of HRC seed and the herbicide the crop is designed to resist. The two principal product lines are currently Monsanto's "Roundup Ready" crops — so-named because they tolerate Monsanto's best-selling herbicide, "Roundup" (glyphosate) — and AgrEvo's "Liberty Link" crops, which tolerate that company's "Liberty" herbicide (glufosinate).

It may sound contradictory, but one ostensible objective of HRCs is to reduce herbicide use. By designing crops that tolerate fairly high levels of exposure to a broad-spectrum herbicide (a chemical that is toxic to a wide range of plants), the companies are giving farmers the option of using a heavy, once-in-the-growing-season dousing with that herbicide, instead of the standard practice, which calls for a series of applications of several different compounds. It's not yet clear whether this new herbicide regime actually reduces the amount of material used, but its simplicity is attracting many farmers to the package....

The bigger problem is that HRCs, like B.t. crops, are really just an extension of the current pesticide paradigm. HRCs may permit a reduction in herbicide use over the short term, but obviously their widespread adoption would encourage herbicide dependency. In many parts of the developing world, where herbicides are not now common, the herbicide habit could mean substantial additional environmental stresses: herbicides are toxic to many soil organisms, they can pollute groundwater, and they may have long-term effects on both people and wildlife.

And of course, resistance will occur. Bob Hartzler, a weed scientist at Iowa State University, warns that if HRCs encourage reliance on just a few broad-spectrum herbicides, then resistance is likely to develop faster — and agriculture is likely to be more vulnerable to it....

## ON THE LOOSE

In 1997, just one year after its first commercial planting in Canada, a farmer reported — and DNA testing confirmed — that Roundup Ready canola had cross-pollinated with a related weed species growing in the field's margins, and produced an herbicide-tolerant descendant. The gene for herbicide resistance had "escaped."

If a transgenic crop is capable of sexual reproduction (and they generally are), the leaking of "transgenes" is to some degree inevitable, if any close relatives are growing in the vicinity. This type of genetic pollution is not likely to be common in the industrialized countries, where most major crops have relatively few close relatives. But in the developing world — especially in regions where a major crop originated — the picture is very different....

There's no way to predict what would happen if the B.t. gene were to escape into a wild flora, but there's good reason to be concerned. John Losey, an entomologist at Cornell University, has been experimenting with Monarch butterflies, by raising their caterpillars on milkweed dusted with B.t.-corn pollen. Losey found that nearly half of the insects raised on this fare died and

90

the rest were stunted. (Caterpillars raised on milkweed dusted with ordinarily corn pollen did fine.) According to Losey, "these levels of mortality are comparable to those you find with especially toxic insecticides." If the gene were to work a change that dramatic in a wild plant's toxicity, then it could trigger a cascade of second- and third-order ecological effects.

The potential for this kind of trouble is likely to grow, since a major interest in biotech product development is "trait-stacking" — combining several engineered genes in a single variety, as with the attempts to develop corn with multiple toxins. Monsanto's "stacked cotton" — Roundup Ready and B.t.-producing — is already on the market in the United States. Eventually, a single crop could diffuse a wide array of potent genes into the wild.

In the agricultural hot spots, there is an important practical reason to be concerned about any resulting genetic pollution. Plant breeders depend on the genetic wealth of the hot spots to maintain the vigor of the major crops — and there's no realistic possibility of biotech rendering this natural wealth "obsolete." But it certainly is possible that foreign genes could upset the relationships between the local varieties and their wild relatives. How would that affect the entire genetic complex? There's probably no way to know until after the fact.

## NEW FEUDALISM

The advent of transgenic crops raises serious social questions as well — beginning with ownership. All transgenic seed is patented, as are most nontransgenic commercial varieties....

The right to own genes is a relatively new phenomenon in world history and its effects on agriculture — and on life in general — are still very uncertain. The biotech companies argue that ownership is essential for driving their industry: without exclusive rights to a product that costs hundreds of millions of dollars to develop, how will it be possible to attract investors? And some industry advocates see patents as a way of "investing" in biodiversity in general.

Patents are clearly an important ingredient in the industry's expansion. Global sales of transgenic crop products grew from $75 million in 1995 to $1.5 billion in 1998 — a 20-fold increase. Sales are expected to hit $25 billion by 2010. And as the market has expanded, so has the scramble for patents....

## THE SIERRA CLUB CALLS FOR...

...Extensive, rigorous research on the potential long-term environmental and health impacts of genetically engineered organisms (GEOs) before they are released into the environment.

Use of the precautionary principle, whereby: (1) harm is avoided before scientific certainty has been established, and (2) the burden of proof is shifted to those with the power and resources to prevent harm.

Mandatory environmental impact statements to be made for every ecosystem into which any new GEO is to be introduced. These should be based on rigorous science and open public debate.

An end to the concept of "substantial equivalence" by our regulatory agencies as a ploy to sidestep safety studies and oversight responsibilities. For example, toxins meant to kill insects are being genetically engineered into plants, yet the consequences of these toxins in the diets of humans, livestock, beneficial insects, and wildlife are unknown....

Excerpted from a letter of Carl Pope on behalf of the Sierra Club available at www.purefood. org/ge/sierraclub.cfm.

But there is far more at stake here than the fortunes of the industry itself: patents and similar legal mechanisms may be giving companies additional control over farmers. As a way of securing their patent rights, biotech companies are requiring farmers to sign "seed contracts" when they purchase transgenic seed — a wholly new phenomenon in agriculture. The contracts may stipulate what brand of pesticides the farmer must use on the crop — a kind of legal cement for those crop-herbicide "technology packages." And the contracts generally forbid the types of activities that had been permitted under the earlier patent regimes.

## SEED SAVING

The most troubling aspect of these contracts is the possible effect on seed saving — the ancient practice of reserving a certain amount of harvested seed for the next planting. In the developing world, some 1.4 billion farmers still rely almost exclusively on seed saving for their planting needs. As a widespread, low-tech form of breeding, seed saving is also critical to the husbandry of crop diversity, since farmers generally save seed from plants that have done best under local conditions. The contracts have little immediate relevance to seed saving in the developing world, since the practice there is employed largely by farmers who could not afford transgenic seed in the first place. But even in industrialized countries, seed saving is still common in certain areas and for certain crops, and Monsanto has already taken legal action against over 300 farmers for replanting proprietary seeds.

The struggle to enforce those broad patents is unlikely to stop with seed contracts — or to remain a First World concern. A recent invention — officially entitled the "gene protection technology" — may make the seed contracts a biological reality. The terminator prevents harvested seeds from germinating. Its principal inventor, a U.S. Department of Agriculture molecular biologist named Melvin Oliver, notes that "the technology primarily targets Second and Third World markets" — in effect guaranteeing patent rights even in nations where patent enforcement is weak or nonexistent. The terminator may also encourage the patenting of some major crops, such as rice, wheat, and sorghum, that have generally been ignored by private-sector breeders. Although there has been a great deal of public-sector development of these crops, it has been difficult for private companies to make money on them, because it is relatively easy for farmers to breed stable, productive varieties on their own. The terminator could allow companies to get a better "grip" on such crops....

## SOCIAL, ENVIRONMENTAL CONSEQUENCES

There is no question that biotech contains some real potential for agriculture, for instance as a supplement to conventional breeding or as a means of studying crop pathogens. But if the industry continues to follow its current trajectory, then biotech's likely contribution will be marginal at best and at worst, given the additional dimensions of ecological and social unpredictability — who knows? In any case, the biggest hope for agriculture is not something biochemists are going to find in a test tube. The biggest opportunities will be found in what farmers already know, or in what they can readily discover on their farms.

READING

# 13

# FOOD FOR THE FUTURE:
## GENETICALLY MODIFIED FOOD AND REGULATORY REASSURANCE

### Dan Glickman

*Dan Glickman is the U.S. Secretary of Agriculture for the Clinton Administration.*

### ■ POINTS TO CONSIDER

1. How does Glickman account for consumer resistance to genetically modified organisms?

2. Discuss the author's comments on food labeling.

3. Identify the connection between consumers and global trade, according to Glickman.

4. List the ways by which the author aims to increase consumer acceptance of genetically modified food.

Excerpted from the address of the U.S. Secretary of Agriculture Dan Glickman before the National Press Club, "New Crops, New Century, New Challenges: How Will Scientists, Farmers and Consumers Learn to Love Biotechnology and What Happens if They Don't?" Washington, D.C., 13 July 1999.

*I have felt for some time that when biotechnology products from agriculture hit the market with attributes that, let's say, reduce cholesterol, consumer acceptance will rise dramatically.*

Let's think about this hypothetical situation for a moment: Let's suppose that today's salad was made with the new carrot from Press Club Farms, Inc. Farmers grow the new carrot on fewer acres because it yields more, and it's less expensive because it does not require any fertilizers or pesticides and can be harvested totally mechanically. In addition, it has more Vitamin A and C than traditional varieties and stays crisper longer and keeps its fresh taste longer.

## TIP OF ICEBERG

But, because this carrot does not require as much labor, the farmers have had to lay off hundreds of employees. While it does not require any chemicals to flourish, this new carrot does affect the environment by making it difficult for other crops or plants in close proximity to survive. And though it's cheaper to begin with, it's only available from one company, which could result in a considerable premium over regular carrot seed.

And what's the secret to this hypothetical new carrot? It's the latest advance from biotechnology — produced with a gene from kudzu, an invasive weed.

Sound far-fetched? It probably shouldn't: Remember the flavor-saver tomato? How many of you have heard of the so-called terminator gene which can keep a plant from reproducing? Today, nearly half the soybeans in the U.S., the stuff that is crushed and made into salad and cooking oil and that feeds most of the livestock we grow, are produced from a variety that increases the plant's resistance to certain pesticides. Genetically engineered corn with certain pest-resistant characteristics is also rapidly displacing more traditional varieties. And, it gets even more interesting when you consider that researchers are looking at genetically modified mosquitoes that cannot carry malaria.

So, what do you think about this new carrot? Are we concerned about the environmental effects we still don't fully understand? What about the farm workers who are now unemployed? Should one company have a monopoly on it? And finally, are you concerned about these issues and about how it is produced? Would you still have eaten it if you knew about the kudzu gene? Should you have been told? Would you buy it?

Folks, this is the tip of the biotechnology iceberg. There are many more questions that haven't yet been thought of, much less answered. But first of all, and if you come away with a dominant point from my remarks, it is that I want you to know that biotechnology has enormous potential.

## RESISTANCE

But, as with any new technology, the road is not always smooth. Right now, in some parts of the world there is great consumer resistance and great cynicism toward biotechnology. In Europe protesters have torn up test plots of biotechnology-derived crops and some of the major food companies in Europe have stopped using genetically modified organisms (GMOs) in their products.

The World Trade Organization (WTO) affirmed our view that the European Union (EU) is unjustifiably blocking U.S. ranchers from selling beef produced with completely tested and safe growth hormones. Today we're seeing that the G-8 agreed to a new review of food safety issues and, I can assure you that trade in GMOs is looming larger over U.S.-EU trade relations in all areas.

Now, more than ever, with these technologies in their relative infancy, I think it's important that, as we encourage the development of these new food production systems, we cannot blindly embrace their benefits. We have to ensure public confidence in general, consumer confidence in particular, and assure farmers that they will benefit.

The important question is not, do we accept the changes the biotechnology revolution can bring, but are we willing to heed the lessons of the past in helping us to harness this burgeoning technology. The promise and potential are enormous, but so, too, are the questions, many of which are completely legitimate. Today, on the threshold of this revolution, we have to grapple with and satisfy those questions so we can in fact fulfill biotechnology's awesome potential.

## ARM'S LENGTH REGULATORY PROCESS

The U.S. regulatory path for testing and commercializing biotechnology products as they move from lab to field to marketplace is over a decade old. We base decisions on rigorous analysis and sound scientific principles. Three federal agencies, U.S. Department of Agriculture (USDA), Food and Drug Administration (FDA), and Environmental Protection Agency (EPA) each place a role in determining the use of biotechnology products in the United States: USDA evaluates products for potential risk to other plants and animals. FDA reviews biotechnology's effect on food safety. And the EPA examines any products that can be classified as pesticides.

Right now, there are about 50 genetically altered plant varieties approved by USDA. And so far, thanks to the hard work and dedication of our scientists, the system is keeping pace. But, as I said, the system is tried and tested, but not perfect and not inviolate and should be improved where and when possible. To meet the future demand of the thousands of products in the pipeline will require even greater resources, and a more unified approach and broader coordination.

When I chaired the U.S. delegation to the World Food Conference in Rome in 1996, I got pelted with genetically modified soybeans by naked protesters. I began to realize the level of opposition and distrust in parts of Europe to biotechnology for products currently on the market or in the pipeline.

I believe that distrust is scientifically unfounded. It comes in part from the lack of faith in the EU to assure the safety of their food. They have no independent regulatory agencies like the FDA, USDA or EPA. They've had many food scares in recent years — mad cow disease, and recently, dioxin-tainted chicken — that have contributed to a wariness of any food that is not produced in a traditional manner notwithstanding what the science says. Ironically they do not share that fear as it relates to genetically modified pharmaceuticals.

But, GMO foods evoke in many circles a very volatile reaction. And that has created a serious problem for the U.S. and other countries as we try to sell our commodities in international markets.

## CONSUMER ACCEPTANCE

However strong our regulatory process is, it is of no use if consumer confidence is low and if consumers cannot identify a direct benefit to them.

I have felt for some time that when biotechnology products from agriculture hit the market with attributes that, let's say, reduce cholesterol, increase disease resistance, grow hair, lower pesticide and herbicide use, and are truly recognized as products that create more specific public benefits, consumer acceptance will rise dramatically.

There's been a lot of discussion as to whether we should label GMO products. There are clearly trade and domestic implications for labeling to be considered in this regard. I know many of us are sorting out these issues. Many observers, including me, believe some type of informational labeling is likely to happen. But, I do believe that it is imperative that such labeling does not undermine trade and this promising new technology.

The concept of labeling particular products for marketing purposes is not a radical one. For example, USDA has already decided that for a product to be certified as "organic" under our pending organic agriculture rules, a GMO product would not qualify. And that does not mean that USDA believes organic is safer or better than non-organic; all approved foods are safe; it just means that consumers are given this informed choice.

## FEAR, DOUBT AND OPPOSITION

There clearly needs to be a strong public education effort to show consumers the benefits of these products and why they are safe. Not only will this be the responsibility of private industry and government, but I think the media will play a vital role. It's important that the media treat this subject responsibly and not sensationalize or fan consumer fears. That's what we're seeing happen in the EU and the outcome is fear, doubt and outright opposition.

What we cannot do is take consumers for granted. I cannot stress that enough. A sort of if-you-grow-it-they-will-come mentality. I believe farmers and consumers will eventually come to see the economic, environmental, and health benefits of biotechnology products, particularly if the industry reaches out and becomes more consumer-accessible.

But, to build consumer confidence, it is just like it is with the way we regulate our airlines, our banks and the safety of our food supply — consumers must have trust in the regulatory process. That trust is built on openness. Federal agencies have nothing to hide. We work on behalf of the public interest. Understanding that will go a long way to solving the budding controversy over labeling and ensuring that consumers will have the ability to make informed choices.

## CORPORATE CITIZENSHIP

If the promises hold true, biotechnology will bring revolutionary benefits to society. But that very promise means that industry needs to be guided by a broader map and not just a compass pointing toward the bottom line.

Product development to date has enabled those who oppose this technology to claim that all the talk about feeding the world is simply cover for corporate profit-making. To succeed in the long term, industry needs to act with greater sensitivity and foresight.

In addition, private-sector research should also include the public interest, with partnerships and cooperation with non-governmental organizations here and in the developing world ensuring that the fruits of this technology address the most compelling needs like hunger and food security.

Biotechnology developers must keep farmers informed of the latest trends, not just in research but in the marketplace as well. Contracts with farmers need to be fair and not result in a system that reduces farmers to mere serfs on the land or create an atmosphere of mistrust among farmers or between farmers and companies.

Companies need to continue to monitor products, after they've gone to market, for potential danger to the environment and maintain open and comprehensive disclosure of their findings. We don't know what biotechnology has in store for us in the future, good and bad, but if we stay on top of developments, we're going to make sure that biotechnology serves society, not the other way around.

These basic principles of good corporate citizenship really just amount to good long-term business practices. As in every other sector of the economy, we expect responsible corporate citizenship and a fair return. For the American people, that is the bottom line.

## FREE AND OPEN TRADE

The issues I have raised have profound consequences in world trade. Right now, we are fighting the battles on ensuring access to our products on many fronts. We are not alone in these battles. Canada, Australia, Mexico, many Latin American, African and Asian nations, agree with us that sound science ought to establish whether biotech products are safe and can move in international commerce.

These are not academic problems. For 1998 crops 44% of our soybeans and 36% of our corn are produced from genetically modified seeds. While only a few varieties of GMO products have been approved for sale and use in Europe, many more have been put on hold by a *de facto* European moratorium on new GMO products.

To forestall a major U.S.-EU trade conflict, both sides of the Atlantic must tone down the rhetoric, roll up our sleeves and work toward conflict resolution based on open trade, sound science and consumer involvement. I think this can be done if the will is there. However, I should warn our friends across the Atlantic that, if these issues cannot be resolved in this manner, we will vigorously fight for our legitimate rights.

## CONCLUSION

So let us continue to move forward thoughtfully with biotechnology in agriculture but with a measured sense of what it is and what it can be. We will then avoid relegating this promising new technology to the pile of what-might-have-beens, and instead realize its potential as one of the tools that will help us feed the growing world population in a sustainable manner.

# FRANKENFOOD:
## GENETICALLY MODIFIED FOOD AND HEALTH CONCERNS

### Jane Kay

*Jane Kay is a staff writer for the* San Francisco Examiner. *She focuses on environmental issues.*

■ **POINTS TO CONSIDER**

1. Describe the monarch butterfly experiments. What significance does this study have on genetically modified food issues?

2. Discuss the concept "Frankenfood." Where did it originate and why?

3. Identify the various consumer fears cited in the article.

4. What concerns do food advocates have with regulatory regimes?

5. Evaluate the precautionary principle set forth by Kay. Does Glickman (see previous reading) employ this?

Excerpted from Jane Kay, "You Say Potato, They Say Pesticide," **San Francisco Examiner,** 11 July 1999. Reprinted by permission, **San Francisco Examiner.**

***The British Medical Association opposed rapid intro-
duction of the crops into Great Britain and advised a
ban on imported foods if they weren't clearly labeled.***

The popcorn at your movie house could be made from plants
designed to fight off a voracious pest called the corn borer. Your
baby's formula could come from soybean plants biologically
transformed to withstand the herbicide Roundup. The bags of
potato chips on your grocer's shelves could be sliced from spuds
containing a gene that poisons Colorado potato beetles.

## GE CONCERNS

A dramatic increase in reliance on genetic engineering (GE)
may be helping produce bumper crops, but it also is raising concern that labeling laws are weak and that too little is known about
potential effects on humans and the environment. As of 1998,
growers in the United States, Argentina, Canada, Australia,
Mexico, Spain, France and South Africa dedicated 69.5 million
acres to genetically modified crops, a 16-fold increase over just
two years, according to the International Service for the
Acquisition of Agri-biotech Applications, an industry institute to
promote new technology.

In the United States, which represents three-fourths of the
world's agricultural acreage, altered corn accounted for 40 percent of the total crop planted in 1999, up from 26.5 percent the
year before. In 1999, for the first time, canola farmers planted
300,000 acres of engineered plants. Acreage devoted to a wide
range of engineered crops from papaya to radicchio to squash is
expanding.

In opposition, consumer groups are citing a startling Cornell
University lab experiment from May 1999 in which pollen from a
corn plant altered to eradicate corn borers killed monarch butterfly larvae. If the butterfly might succumb, they reason, what might
happen to humans who consume a lifelong diet of such crops?
And what might happen to beneficial insects and wildlife in the
environment? The questions are pitting consumers against the
agricultural industry and the U.S. government, which insist that
food from genetically modified crops, primarily corn, soybeans,
cotton and potatoes, is no different and requires no special tests or
labels.

# FRANKENFOOD

Opposition is swelling in Europe, where the term "Frankenfood" has entered the lexicon; some major supermarket and fast-food chains have promised to rid themselves of the products; and Italy, Greece, France, Luxembourg and Denmark are blocking authorization of new genetic crops in fields and markets of European Union nations.

The resistance may be spreading. "U.S. consumers, too, are demanding mandatory labeling and mandatory testing for environmental and human health effects," said biologist Michael Hansen, research associate at Consumers Union's Consumer Policy Institute.

The biotechnology industry, led by Monsanto, Novartis, Dow, DuPont, AgrEvo and Zeneca, calls rising criticism in Europe "hysteria and hype" from the food scare over "mad cow" disease in England and dioxin in feed, poultry, beef and butter in Belgium....

Genetic engineering has come into practice over the last 20 years. Most commonly, bacteria, viruses, and genes from tobacco or petunia plants are inserted into soy, corn, cotton and canola so that plants can survive field applications of weed killers. Or a gene from *Bacillus thuringiensis,* or B.t., a bacteria found in soil, is inserted into corn, cotton and potatoes to produce a protein toxic to pests that feed on them.

# A NEED FOR LABELING?

Numerous polls over the past four years have revealed consumer demand for labeling of genetically modified foods, a step the industry is fighting. The last survey by the U.S. Department of Agriculture (USDA), conducted on 604 New Jersey residents in 1995, found that 84 percent of those polled wanted mandatory labeling of engineered fruits and vegetables. In interviews, major food companies, Frito-Lay, General Mills, Gerber, Heinz, Kraft, Nabisco, Pillsbury, Procter & Gamble, Quaker and Ross Products Division of Abbott Laboratories said they accepted genetically engineered ingredients for their food products. But consumers can't go into stores or call industry trade groups to secure a list of engineered brands, complains *GeneWatch,* a bulletin of the Council for Responsible Genetics, a Cambridge, Mass., nonprofit organization. "People have a right to know what they're buying in a transaction," said Philip Bereano, a professor of technical communication at the University of Washington who writes for *GeneWatch*. "They have a right to spend their dollars in accordance with their preferences, even if their preferences were irrational," Bereano said. The companies have lobbied successfully against labels before the U.S. Food and Drug Administration (FDA), which regulates food additives, and the U.S. Environmental Protection Agency (EPA), which regulates pesticides....

In May 1992, then-Vice President Dan Quayle announced a long-awaited U.S. policy: Genetically engineered crops, judged by government scientists to be no different from plants bred traditionally, would need no extra government scrutiny. The processed food made from the crops wouldn't require labeling or special testing before going to market.

The FDA doesn't test bio-engineered foods before they go to the public, deeming them not "materially" different from other foods. If the foods later pose a risk to public health, the FDA has the authority to remove them from the marketplace. FDA representatives say they would require labeling only if genes from plants that could cause allergies were engineered into a crop. "The only way to be assured of not consuming genetically engineered food is to only buy food that is certified with an organic labeling," Bereano said.

## POTATO AS PESTICIDE

Some foods, such as Monsanto's New Leaf potato, are actually registered with the EPA as pesticides; every part of it can kill a Colorado potato beetle. As a result, it comes under the regulatory jurisdiction of the EPA, not the Food and Drug Administration. Kathleen Knox, deputy director of EPA's Biopesticides and Pollution Prevention Division, said the agency "regulates biopesticides as we regulate other pesticides. We do the equivalent that we do for any other pesticides."

In the case of the bacterium B.t., she said, "We believe it's safe in the food supply. We certainly have looked at many factors, and we make sure things are adequately tested, particularly the things we've registered so far. We've collected data, done risk assessments. We continue to monitor what's going on in the field."

Hansen, of the Consumer Policy Institute, said neither the EPA,

Illustration by Kitty Kennedy. Reprinted with permission.

the FDA nor the USDA required adequate testing. "If you look at the FDA requirements carefully, you'll see that the industry is on the honor system," Hansen said. "There is no mandatory safety testing of food before it's put on the market. B.t. crops aren't even regulated by the FDA. Legally, those crops aren't considered food but pesticides, which are regulated by the EPA."

But the EPA doesn't test the safety of the engineered plant itself, the potato with B.t. in it, Hansen said. The EPA tests B.t. in isolation. Further, the studies are flawed because they don't use the B.t. toxin produced by the plant but use the B.t. toxin produced by engineered bacteria, which is different, he said.

Critics say inserting a gene into a living cell is highly imprecise, with no control over where in the DNA the new gene is implanted. This can disrupt the natural genetic information encoded in the DNA of a new plant, leading to unexpected and unwanted effects, including potentially increasing toxin levels, changing nutritional values or introducing allergy-causing properties. "When you insert a gene into DNA by using genetic modification, you have no idea where the gene goes; it's absolutely a shot in the dark," said molecular biologist John Fagan, founder of Genetic ID, Inc., a Fairfield, Iowa, laboratory. The lab tests foods for the presence of genetically engineered materials. His clients include many large food retailers in Europe that have promised to start weeding out modified foods. "These random mutagenic events can cause plants or crops to produce new toxins, new allergens or they can reduce the nutritional value of the food," Fagan said. Because the toxins or other properties may be new, he said, there's no way to predict their effects. "The only way to detect them will be actual feeding studies with paid human volunteers," he said. "They do this for drugs and new food additives, and yet these tests are not required of the agricultural biotechnology industry. The FDA's own scientists have expressed serious concerns about this." New studies are raising questions, said Fagan, who for nearly 20 years, including seven years at the National Institutes of Health, has used genetic engineering techniques in basic research.

## NUTRITIONAL VALUE

A preliminary study by the Center for Ethics and Toxics in the North Coast town of Gualala, published July 1, 1999, in the *Journal of Medicinal Food,* found that soybeans altered to withstand Roundup might be nutritionally inferior to conventional soybeans. The altered soybeans contain reduced levels of phytoestrogens, substances in plants that are credited with guarding against heart disease and cancer, among other health benefits. In a 1998 preliminary study at Rowett Research Institute in Aberdeen, Scotland, rats fed genetically modified potatoes suffered damaged organs and stunted growth compared with rats eating normal potatoes.

A review panel formed by the Royal Society, a scientific body, challenged the research. Researcher Arpad Pusztai has said the panel hadn't looked at his recent data.

## LOOK BEFORE YOU LEAP

Critics complain there is little study on the environmental effects of genetically altered plants. The Cornell University experiment was an exception. "That tiny little monarch butterfly experiment, one that any high school student could have done? Well, those studies weren't being done," said Ignacio Chapel, Assistant Professor in the Department of Environmental Science, Policy and Management at University of California-Berkeley. Researchers report that two beneficial insects that attack pests, ladybugs and green lacewings, also might be victims of the crops designed to kill the corn borer and the Colorado potato beetle.

The Swiss Federal Research Station for Agroecology and

## ANTIBIOTIC RESISTANCE

Some genetically manipulated plants already grown today contain genes which render antibiotics ineffective. These antibiotic-resistant genes can be absorbed by pathogenic bacteria in human or animal intestines, and can then no longer be combated by the relevant antibiotics. The Novartis company's genetically modified maize, which was first grown in Europe in 1998 and can already be processed and used in food, should be regarded particularly critically. This maize contains a gene resistant to diverse penicillins frequently used in human medicine. There is a direct danger to health in using such plants as feedstuff or food. They must therefore be banned....

GreenPeace, "Antibiotic Resistance in Genetically Modified Plants," available at www.greenpeace.org/_geneng/.

Agriculture found in 1998 that green lacewings suffered a two-thirds increase in death rate when they fed on army worms eating corn engineered to contain a bacteria toxic to crop pests. The Scottish Crop Research Institute in Dundee concluded the same year that female ladybugs that ate aphids that had fed on genetically modified potatoes laid fewer eggs and lived only half as long as the average ladybugs.

In May 1999, the British Medical Association warned that it was far too early to know whether genetically modified foods were safe. It opposed rapid introduction of the crops into Great Britain and advised a ban on imported foods if they weren't clearly labeled. "We should follow the old public health tradition now being used in Europe, called the precautionary principle, which embodies the age-old wisdom of 'look before you leap,'" said Bereano, of *GeneWatch*. "If there's a lot of uncertainty, the prudent course of action is to assess the product before sending it out for mass consumption. The burden of proof should rest on the proponent of the new technology."

READING

# 15

# BIOTECHNOLOGY TO FEED THE WORLD

## Dennis T. Avery

*Dennis T. Avery is a Senior Fellow of the Hudson Institute and Director of the Institute's Center on Global Food Issues. From 1980-88, he served as the senior agricultural analyst for the U.S. Department of State, where he assessed the foreign policy implications of global food and farming developments.*

## ■ POINTS TO CONSIDER

1. List the achievements of high-yield agriculture, according to Avery.

2. Evaluate the author's argument that agricultural biotechnology will save wild lands.

3. Consider Avery's list of past triumphs of high-yield agriculture; why does he believe biotechnology is needed?

4. According to the author, biotechnology in agriculture will aid the Third World. Why? What policy goals should we have toward the Third World?

Excerpted from Dennis T. Avery, **Biodiversity: Saving Species with Biotechnology,** (Hudson Institute Executive Briefing), Indianapolis: Hudson Institute, 1993. Reprinted by permission, Hudson Institute.

*Could we keep the food supply expanding with just the old productivity stalwarts such as plant breeding, irrigation, and fertilizer? Enter biotechnology, stage right.*

...The world does not need to lose its wildlife species or condemn billions of humans to death.

We *do* need to continue our successful pursuit of high-yield agriculture and our new achievements in the world's first high-yield forestry. These two technologies should enable us to feed, clothe, and house twice as many people in 2050, while using less land than we use today.

## DOUBLING THE FOOD SUPPLY

Remember that high-yield agriculture is no pipe dream. Since 1960 it has *already* doubled the world's food production and tripled the productivity of the land and water used in farming. That's why we are now feeding twice as many people *from the same amount of land as we cultivated in 1960!*

Moreover, contrary to the claims of environmental activists, virtually all of this gain in food production has been ecologically sustainable. In fact, it is the activists' favorite alternative, low-yield farming, that is *unsustaining* and therefore unsustainable. It risks humanity *and* wildlife because it cannot support the impending human population without requiring that people plow down vast amounts of wildlife habitat.

People around the world should be applauding high-yield farming as an environmental triumph. It is currently protecting ten million square miles of wildlife habitat. And it is doing so without spending a dime of anybody's money, coerced or otherwise. If the Audubon Society could make such a claim, its directors would be in Stockholm collecting Nobel prizes. Unfortunately, advocates of high-yield agriculture have allowed misguided environmental activists to paint them as ecological villains.

## KEY TO FOOD GAINS

We used to have one big question about high-yield agriculture: Could we keep the food supply expanding with just the old productivity stalwarts such as plant breeding, irrigation, and fertilizer?

Enter biotechnology, stage right. We now know that biotechnology can provide the food and forestry productivity we need to protect the earth's ecology and its biodiversity. Here's how:

**First**, biotechnology will renew the momentum of plant and animal genetics, the key to most of the food production gains achieved so far. Biotech will speed the breeding process, permit the cost-effective production of natural organic compounds, and enormously expand the gene pool available to researchers.

**Second**, biotechnology will give us high-yield forestry to accompany our high-yield agriculture. Cloning and tissue culture have already shortened the tree-breeding cycle from decades to months. This speed-up is producing fourfold increases in the yields of tree crops ranging from rubber and cocoa to teak and pulpwood. When we start actually adding genes to trees, we'll be able to raise forest plantation yields even more rapidly. Thus foresters will be able to produce the forest products needed by ten billion humans on far fewer acres of forest plantations than are used today. We will then be able to leave the vast majority of the world's forests untouched and wild. And remember: the genetic diversity in the plantations is not our main concern; the key is the species preserved in the vast tracts of wild acres that will be left untouched.

## CONSERVATION, BIODIVERSITY

**Third**, biotech will make wild genes vastly more valuable, thus strongly encouraging species conservation. Until now, the odds against finding a useful gene or compound in the wild forest have been a million to one. Until biotech, scientists couldn't use most of the wild genes in the earth's biosphere. Conventional breeding can only crossbreed "first cousins," and most organic chemicals have been too complex to manufacture. With biotech, however, researchers can selectively insert genes from virtually any species anywhere. Complex organic chemicals can be cost-effectively produced by programming laboratory bacteria with the natural gene codes to make them.

If wild genes suddenly become valuable for research, and forest products become cheap because of the great productivity of genetically engineered tree plantations, who will want to cut down wild forests?

**Fourth,** biotechnology will create important new biodiversity. This is not to say that creating a new bacterium for brewing yeast offsets the loss of wild species. Instead, the new organisms will meet some critical needs for both people and the ecology. For example, researchers report that they have already saved the American chestnut tree from chestnut blight and the American elm from Dutch elm disease. That is, either they have saved these species or they have created two important new shade tree species that are each one gene different from the chestnut and the elm, as E.O. Wilson and Paul Ehrlich might argue. In addition, researchers look forward to creating enhanced bacteria that will eat up oil spills and convert them to beneficial compounds.

## REDUCING CHEMICALS

**Fifth,** biotechnology is our best bet to reduce the need for spraying farm chemicals around the environment. Today's fertilizers and pesticides present a health plus for humans. They produce more and lower-cost fruits and vegetables, which reduce risks of cancer and heart disease. These fertilizers and pesticides present minimal danger to the environment when used properly. Nonetheless, if some people still want to get rid of farm chemicals on general principles, they should support biotechnology. Biotech will allow scientists to engineer pest resistance into plants and animals, create new vaccines against diseases, create pheromone traps and sterile insects to disrupt pests' breeding cycles, and much more.

We are already field-testing biotech cotton and corn varieties that produce their own natural biological pest-killer (*Bacillus thuringiensis*). Over time, we will be able to put a wide range and series of pest protections into our plants and animals. We may also be able to provide the same kinds of protection for our pets, to prevent problems such as heartworm and rabies.

## POPULATION

**Sixth,** all this biotechnology should also help speed the increase of affluence in the Third World. And *affluence is the only sure way to achieve zero population growth.* People in very poor countries don't want birth control, because children are among the few assets available to them. Kids are almost immediately useful in the fields and handicrafts, and children are the only social security. Parents living in primitive conditions never have any way of knowing how

## FEEDING AFRICA

...The United Nations' Food and Agricultural Organization estimates that witchweeds alone cause more than 100 million farmers to lose half their already reduced yields. Couple that with government policies of keeping local agricultural prices artificially low, and you get a bleak picture of a yield-reducing spiral: farmers find it unprofitable to buy quality crop seeds, use fertilizers, or care about the quality of weeding. Agricultural biotechnology can offer the means to reverse that spiral....

Using biotechnologically engineered herbicide-resistant corn seeds and then soaking the seeds in those herbicides could provide a simple "quick fix." The parasites will unwittingly devour the weed-killing chemical from the roots or surrounding soil and die. By the time the crops ripen, the herbicide will be gone and will not affect the food supply....

Jonathan Gressel, "Plant Biotechnology Can Quickly Offer Solutions to Hunger in Africa," **The Scientist,** 30 September 1996.

many of their kids will die before them. In contrast, there has never been an affluent country with a continuing high birth rate. In a rich country, kids are an expensive ego investment.

Third World economic and ecological improvements are especially critical to the environment. The activists are wrong when they claim that the First World is the major pollution problem. The First World was simply the *initial* pollution problem. Most Third World residents have already reached the most highly polluting stage of development. They already live in filthy cities that burn coal, smelt iron, and don't treat their sewage.

The rich countries, by contrast, are now past the worst polluting phase. They treat their sewage, put tight controls on industrial effluents, cut soil erosion to near-zero levels, and protect wildlife species even when it costs people their jobs. They also do the research on critical environmental problems and the best ways to resolve them.

The biggest environmental challenge of the future is in Asia and the tropics, not North America and Europe. And the solution to the problem *must* include high-yield agriculture and forestry.

"Population management" won't come fast enough to protect today's wild species — unless it means deliberately starving billions of people. Population stability through affluence is still several decades away. Where population growth and wildlife really are in conflict, the wildlife is losing. Consider, for example, the elephants and gorillas in Africa, where primitive tribes are extending low-yield agriculture into their habitats.

## ENCOURAGING RESEARCH AND GROWTH

High-yield agriculture is already available and is our best solution to the conflict. Unfortunately, the First World is cutting back its support for agricultural research, just as the world is beginning the biggest food-demand surge in its history. We are being misled by foolish, government-induced farm surpluses and the environmental movement's pleas for low-yield organic farming.

How many millions of square miles of wildlife habitat are the environmental activists willing to plow down to pay for their chemical-free farming?

Many environmental activists are trying to block biotechnology also — the one approach that can make it easy and profitable to save forests and wildlife. Rather than exploit this rich intellectual terrain, they want to mandate forest preservation through government regulations — mostly in trackless regions where government enforcement is next to impossible.

In fact, the environmental movement's favorite bogeymen — the big chemical companies — are the ones who have invested the most money in biotechnology. And these biotech investments can do more for the environment  than all the nature preserves ever dreamt of by the Sierra Club.

To protect our biodiversity, we must do two things:

- We must pursue more scientific solutions, especially biotechnology, for the major categories of world land use. Zero population growth won't come fast enough to save our biodiversity by itself.

- Far from suppressing economic growth, we must encourage it, so that a richer world will rapidly achieve lower birth rates and be able to invest in scientific studies and technological advances that can conserve the environment. Biotech will help with that, too.

# SUSTAINABLE AGRICULTURE TO FEED TO WORLD

## Jules Pretty

*Jules Pretty is Director of the Center for Environment and Society at the Univesity of Essex. He is the author of* The Living Land: Agriculture, Food and Community in Rural Europe.

## ■ POINTS TO CONSIDER

1. Rather than lack of food production, what factors does the author identify as the cause of hunger?

2. How does the author view the claims of biotech companies? Does he believe biotechnology will feed the world's hungry?

3. Identify the achievements of sustainable agriculture, according to Pretty.

4. What agricultural policy goals does the author support?

Excerpted from Jule Pretty, "Strange Fruit," **RedPepper,** November 1998 Reprinted by permission of the author.

*We know sustainable farming can greatly improve the productivity of the land. It has already done so for more than two million families in the past five to ten years.*

Ever since the advent of farming, there has been a constant struggle to make sure that enough food is produced on farms to feed everyone. This challenge has become ever more acute in the last half of this century. Even though we can put people on the moon, we simply cannot seem to find a way to make sure that everyone gets at least enough food to eat. And the problem will get worse before it gets better. The world population stands at six billion people. It will eventually stabilize somewhere between eight and eleven billion. Most of this growth will occur in the poorer countries of the world. Today, a seventh of all the world's people are hungry — all 800 million of them. This much is agreed, but what we do about it is highly contested. We know food production will have to increase, otherwise we could be faced with crises of epic proportions.

But it is not a simple problem. We actually produce enough food in the world to feed everyone with a nutritious and adequate diet now — on average 350 kg. of cereal per person. A good deal of cereal is turned into meat, milk and other animal products, which in energy terms is inefficient. But a more important factor is that most hungry people are poor, and they simply do not have the money to buy the food they need. Poor farmers cannot afford expensive "modern" technologies that could increase their yields. What they need are readily available and cheap means to improve their farms. Surprisingly, there are signs that a quiet revolution in the world food system is beginning to occur. Not all agree. Many currently are saying that genetic modification of our crops and animals is a necessary condition for feeding the world. But is it?

## IS GENETIC MODIFICATION THE ANSWER?

Those concerned with the food system, from farmers to consumers, from activists to companies, from citizens to policy makers, neatly fall into very different camps. These "schools of thought" shape the way policy makers think about the problem, and what we might want to do about it. Some say that it will have to be the industrialized countries that come to the rescue by greatly increasing their own farm production. Others say that exporting fertilizers and pesticides to developing countries will help them increase their production. Others still advocate genetic modification of plants and animals as the greatest single technology that will feed the world. Another group says that sustainable agriculture is a viable alternative for all farmers, whether in developing or developed countries, as it has the potential to greatly improve productivity on existing lands.

At first glance, none of these may seem contentious. It could be that each has its place, and can make a contribution. But regrettably, some of the protagonists are conveniently ignoring the contributions of others. What are some of these myth-makers saying? One of the biggest advocates for genetically engineered crops is the American company, Monsanto. Their public relations campaign, "Let the Harvest Begin" (sic), states that Europeans should stop being selfish in refusing to accept genetically modified organisms (GMOs) because they are a luxury our hungry world cannot afford. They say that agricultural biotechnology will play a major role in realizing the hope we all share. Accepting this science can make a dramatic difference in millions of lives.

One reason why this myth seems to fit our preconceptions is that we still tend to see people in developing countries as victims. Clare Short, the Minister for International Development, asked the media to focus more on positive images and stories rather than only picking up on the disasters. Let's get something straight. The huge numbers of people in severe poverty and suffering continuous hunger is a dreadful indictment on all of us. Something must be done. But that something is not to say we must pursue a path of "modern" technologies and hang the consequences.

Like all new technologies, there are emergent problems associated with biotechnology and genetic engineering. Some of these are fundamental ethical issues — should genes really be transferred across species that do not naturally breed? What kinds of unexpected traits will get transferred along with desired ones? Should human or animal embryos be used for laboratory experimentation? Increased knowledge about genes may lead to the emergence of different genetic classes, and of insurance companies issuing life policies only for people with or without certain genes. Other problems are environmental, and center on concerns over various forms of genetic pollution. Genetically modified (GM) crops could cross-pollinate with weedy relatives to produce superweeds. Insect pests could rapidly develop resistance in the face of large-scale planting of GM crops with insecticidal properties. New virulent strains of viruses or bacteria could emerge.

## BENEFITS FOR THE HUNGRY?

Nonetheless, to condemn the whole field would be to prevent some highly beneficial technologies, for which there are no alternatives, from being used — such as treatment for cystic fibrosis, or the development of virus-resistant rice and cassava varieties, or nematode-resistant bananas. On the other hand, to say or imply that the ethical and environmental dimensions should be entirely set aside because of the immense potential benefits is to miss the opportunity to set sensible limits on the technologies. It is possible that GM crops could make a contribution to food production in developing countries — but only if the technologies are produced by public-interest bodies which make the technologies readily available to poor farmers. Organizations seeking a quick and large return on a technology (such as companies and some research organizations) cannot possibly argue that they are working directly to benefit the 800 million hungry people in the world. And what about their plans for using so-called "terminator technology"? These are seeds that die after one year so that farmers cannot save the seed and use it again. Will these really benefit the two billion people in developing countries currently relying on largely "unimproved" agricultural systems? Who will feed all those people in developing countries? The answer to this question is simple — farmers in those countries, using sustainable methods of production.

## SUSTAINABLE AGRICULTURE

Quietly, slowly and very significantly, sustainable agriculture is sweeping the farming systems of the world. Put simply, it is farming that makes the best use of nature's goods and services while not damaging the environment. It does this by integrating natural processes such as nutrient cycling, nitrogen soil regeneration and pest predators into food production processes. It minimizes the use of non-renewable inputs (pesticides and fertilizers) that damage the environment or harm the health of farmers and consumers. And it makes better use of the knowledge and skills of farmers, so improving their self-reliance and capacities.

During this century, modern agriculture has seen external inputs of pesticides, inorganic fertilizer, animal feedstuffs, energy, tractors and other machinery become the primary means to increase food production. These external inputs, though, have substituted for free natural control processes and resources. Pesticides have replaced biological, cultural and mechanical methods for controlling pests, weeds and diseases; inorganic fertilizers have substituted for livestock manures, composts, nitrogen-fixing crops and fertile soils; and fossil fuels have substituted for locally generated energy sources.

The basic challenge for sustainable agriculture is to maximize the use of locally available and renewable resources. This sounds good — but does it work? The best evidence comes from those very countries of Africa, Asia and Latin America that are said to need "modern" technologies most. Where whole communities have been involved in the complete redesign of farming and other local economic activities, the sustainability dividend is very large. The regenerative technologies and practices are hugely beneficial for both farmers and rural environments. They make a positive contribution to nature.

At the same time, direct costs are reduced. There is "more from less." More natural capital from fewer external inputs, more food output from fewer fossil fuel-derived inputs. These improvements are of two basic types. First, sustainable farming is taking root in the resource-poor areas, those that have remained largely untouched by modern technologies of the past 40 years. Here the dividend is greatly increased food output per hectare — up by two- to three-fold. The second spread is occurring in the higher input systems where the so-called "Green Revolution" has already had an impact on food output, but where there are concerns that yield increases have slowed or stopped and where high use of pesticides causes damage to human health and environments. Here the dividend comes from a greatly reduced use of pesticides — they are replaced by natural predators, habitat redesign, multiple cropping and the like — while increasing yields by a small amount, typically one percent.

## HIGHLIGHTS

What is remarkable is that most of this has happened in the past five to ten years. Moreover, many of the improvements are occurring in remote and resource-poor areas that had been assumed to be incapable of producing food surpluses. Here are some highlights:

- Some 223,000 farmers in southern Brazil using green manures and cover crops of legumes and livestock integration have doubled yields of maize and wheat to four to five tons per hectare.

- Some 45,000 farmers in Guatemala and Honduras have used regenerative technologies to triple maize yields to two to two and a half tons per hectare and diversify their upland farms, which has led to local economic growth that has in turn encouraged re-migration back from the cities.

- More than 300,000 farmers in southern and western India farming in dryland conditions, and now using a range of water and soil management technologies, have tripled sorghum and millet yields to two to two and a half tons per hectare.

- Some 200,000 farmers across Kenya, as part of various government and non-government soil and water conservation and sustainable agriculture programs, have more than doubled their maize yields to about 2.5 to 3.3 tons per hectare and substantially improved vegetable production through the dry seasons.

- 100,000 small coffee farmers in Mexico have adopted fully organic production methods, and yet increased yields by half.

- A million wetland rice farmers in Bangladesh, China, India, Indonesia, Malaysia, Philippines, Sri Lanka, Thailand and Vietnam have shifted to sustainable agriculture, where group-based farmer-field schools have enabled farmers to learn alternatives to pesticides while still increasing their yields by about ten percent.

In addition to these, there are many smaller-scale successes. In "unfashionable" countries like Burkina Faso, Ethiopia, Senegal, Uganda and Zambia, like Bolivia and Peru, like China and Pakistan, many thousands of community-level initiatives are now showing that if farmers are involved in technology development, then they can substantially improve the food outputs from farming without diminishing natural capital. Far from being unfashionable, many of these countries are pointing to a new future — one in which there is sufficient food for all, produced in ways that do not damage the environment.

## SCARE TACTICS

What is the expected response of farmers in industrialized countries to sustainable agriculture? The story is that if they were to adopt sustainable farming, then food yields would fall so much that the world food system itself would be under threat. At the beginning of the 1990s, the former U.S. Secretary of Agriculture, Earl Butz, said we could move to more sustainable farming, but "before we move in that direction, someone must decide which fifty million of our people will starve. We simply cannot feed, even at subsistence levels, our 250 million Americans without a large production input of chemicals, antibiotics and growth hormones."

This view is simply nonsense, as it once again ignores what is happening right now. In a study for my new book *The Living Land,* I looked at projects in seven industrialized countries of Europe and North America, and found that remarkable changes are underway. Farmers are finding that they can cut their inputs of costly pesticides and fertilizers substantially, varying from 20-80 percent, and be financially better off. Yields do fall to begin with (by 10-15 percent typically), but there is compelling evidence that they soon rise and go on increasing. In the U.S., for example, the top quarter of sustainable agriculture farmers now have higher yields than conventional farmers, as well as a much lower negative impact on the environment.

The challenge is still massive. We know sustainable farming can greatly improve the productivity of the land. It has already done so for more than two million families in the past five to ten years. Yet there is still a very long way to go.

## DIRECTING PUBLIC POLICY

It is vital that we do all we can to build the capacities of farmers and countries to make improvements with sustainable agriculture. This will need us to get the policies right — only one country in the world has an explicit policy promoting sustainable agriculture over alternatives, and that is Cuba. We will need to get our international development aid right. Britain is taking a lead in the international community with its recent reforms set out in the *1997 White Paper on International Development*. And we will need to inform our citizens about what is happening, so that they can form fair judgments on the alternatives we may or may not seek to promote in the name of "feeding the world."

A key action that governments should now take is to declare a national policy for sustainable agriculture. This would help to raise the profile of these processes and needs, as well as giving explicit value to alternative societal goals. However, even without such a national strategy, policy makers have found that sustainability can begin to be furthered in agriculture by taking steps both to penalize polluters and to encourage resource conservers.

There is a growing sense that green or eco-taxes are an efficient way to help meet environmental objectives, as well as to generate jobs and raise government revenue. These shift the burden of taxation away from economic "goods," such as labor and sales, towards environmental "bads," such as energy, transport, waste and pollution. The market prices of food and other agricultural products do not reflect the full costs of the farming and food system as it currently operates. Some of these costs are not borne by the producer but dispersed through society. The producer does not need to pay for them and so has lower costs. Environmental taxes or pollution payments, however, seek to "internalize" some of these costs, so encourages individuals and businesses to use resources more efficiently. Green taxes, therefore, are a double dividend option. They could cut environmental damage while promoting welfare. National taxes on pesticides seem the most likely option in Britain. But, of course, there are very real constraints to overcome. Vested interests in maintaining the *status quo* will make any change difficult. Why should fertilizer companies support a transition to legume-based livestock farming when this could cost them several hundred million pounds each year in Britain? Why should a pesticide company be balanced in its presentation of sustainable agriculture, when it knows that this would mean that little or none of its producers will be used? Much will depend on what policy makers and the public appreciate is possible with sustainable approaches to farming, and just what kind of benefits could accrue.

READING

# 17

# CRACK FOR COWS: rbGH AND HUMAN HEALTH

## *Multinational Monitor* with Ronnie Cummins

*Ronnie Cummins is the Director of the Campaign for Food Safety based in Little Marais, Minnesota. Cummins is among those leading an effort to plan a global campaign against Monsanto Corporation. The* Multinational Monitor *is a journal of corporate and social critique.*

### ■ POINTS TO CONSIDER

1. What is rbGH? Describe the author's feelings about rbGH.

2. According to the author, identify the health problems suffered by cows injected with rbGH.

3. Discuss the relationship between rbGH and human health, according to Cummins. How does the author explain rbGH's regulatory approval in the U.S.?

4. What accounts for the difference in attitude between Europe and North America on genetic engineering, in Cummins' estimation? Why do biotechnology and animals present a particularly distasteful reaction in Europe?

5. Evaluate Cummins' view on milk labeling. How does he explain the biotechnology industry's views on product labeling?

Excerpted from "Campaigning for Food Safety: An Interview with Ronnie Cummins," **Multinational Monitor,** December 1998. Reprinted with permission, **Multinational Monitor.**

## rbGh is important because it is the first product of genetic engineering.

**...Multinational Monitor: What is rbGH and why do you think it should be banned from the market?**

**Cummins:** Bovine growth hormone is a genetically engineered animal drug that Monsanto developed. It mimics a chemical hormone that occurs naturally in a cow's body. When you shoot up a milk cow with Monsanto's rbGH, it forces the cow to produce excess quantities of a potent chemical messenger called IGF-1, which in turn forces it to give 15 to 25 percent more milk.

We call rbGh "crack for cows," because when you shoot up cows with rbGH, it revs up their system in such a way that it causes major stress on the cows, major animal health problems. The government admits that there are 22 serious health problems in cows that result from shooting them up with this drug.

When you shoot up cows with this drug, the animals suffer a much higher rate of mastitis — which is an infection of the udder. Dairy farmers then shoot up the cows with more antibiotics to fight off the infection, and many of the antibiotics end up as residues in the milk, because the U.S. government does not have an adequate system for monitoring the antibiotic residues in the milk.

It is for that reason that the U.S. Government Accounting Office recommended to the Food and Drug Administration (FDA), both in 1992 and 1993, that it not approve this drug. They said, "We've already got a problem with excessive antibiotic residues in our milk supply and, if you legalize rbGH, the problem is going to get much worse."

The first concern regarding human health hazards is increased antibiotic residues in dairy products. The second major hazard is IGF-1. There is mounting scientific evidence that humans who have high levels of IGF-1 in their blood stream are more susceptible to breast cancer, prostate cancer and colon cancer.

**Multinational Monitor: If this is the case, then why did the U.S. government approve it?**

**Cummins:** It appears that the reason the U.S. government approved the drug is because of a rampant conflict of interest in the Clinton Administration with the Monsanto Corporation.

Cartoon by Andrew Singer. Reproduced by permission.

The top scientists at the FDA at the time they were approving rbGH had previously worked for Monsanto as researchers. And the top decision maker at the FDA on approval and labeling, Michael Taylor, previously worked for the King and Spalding law firm, which has Monsanto and its subsidiary Searle as major clients. After Taylor left the FDA he once again went back to work for King and Spalding.

**Multinational Monitor:** *If you go out and buy gallon of milk, what are the chances that the milk comes from an rbGH-treated cow?*

**Cummins:** The chances are pretty good because approximately seven or eight percent of all U.S. dairy cows are being shot up with this drug every two weeks. And since non-organic milk is typically pooled — genetically engineered milk is being co-mingled with the regular milk — you have most people getting at least trace doses of rbGH in their milk and dairy products — unless they are buying organic dairy products or products certified and labeled "rbGH-free."

**Multinational Monitor:** *But it is not just rbGH that disturbs you about Monsanto.*

**Cummins:** Monsanto has a 100-year history of producing toxic chemicals, such as Agent Orange, PCBs and NutraSweet, poisoning workers, polluting communities and then avoiding liability. In Washington, D.C., it has been a prime lobbyist for so-called tort reform — limiting the damages from those poisoned by chemical corporations and other polluters. And Monsanto is the world leader in trying to force genetically engineered foods and crops down the throats of consumers around the world. rbGH is important because it is the first product of genetic engineering. It was commercialized in the United States in 1994. But since then there have been 37 other genetically engineered products approved in the United States and a couple of dozen in places like Canada, Japan and Europe.

The majority of these new genetically engineered products have been commercialized by Monsanto. These include crops such as the Roundup-resistant soybeans, cotton and corn; B.t. cotton and B.t. corn, which have a pesticidal soil microorganism, B.t., spliced right into them; and genetically engineered tomatoes and rapeseed (canola) plants.

Monsanto has been the most vocal of a handful of companies across the globe pushing this technology. Others include DuPont, Novartis, AgrEvo, Dow, Eli Lilly and Zeneca....

**Multinational Monitor: *Why does popular resistance to genetically engineered foods appear stronger in Europe than in the United States?***

**Cummins:** The European resistance to genetically engineered foods has been so strong, first of all, because of the horrific historical experience of the Europeans with genetic engineering during the Nazi era. When Monsanto or Dow gene engineers pop up and say they are going to create a master race of plants, Europeans are not that impressed. Europeans also have a more heightened consciousness regarding out-of-control technologies because of recent nuclear plant accidents like Chernobyl and the advanced state of environmental destruction in areas such as Eastern Europe. So, people are more skeptical about Big Science over there.

Secondly, Europe, since 1996, has gone through a food crisis triggered by the "mad cow" epidemic in Great Britain and other countries. Consumers have learned in Europe that industrialized food production, in this case, feeding back dead and diseased animals on an industrial scale to animals, has unleashed a deadly and incurable brain-wasting disease called CJD, which is the human equivalent of mad cow disease. Even though only 30 or 40 people have died from this particular disease, scientists in the United Kingdom are still warning that it could reach hundreds of thousands or even millions before this epidemic runs its course. So, people are very concerned about what is going into their food.

Finally, the media in Europe have publicized the debate over food safety and genetic engineering much more thoroughly than in the United States. In the United States, if you ask someone on the street about genetically engineered food, probably the only "Frankenfood" they have ever heard of is the bovine growth hormone. When the U.S. media did publicize the rbGH controversy in 1994 and 1995, there was a tremendous upsurge in consumer concern about this, there were protests and milk dumps all over the country, 325 dairies pledged to not use rbGH, there were hearings in Congress, a bill was introduced in Congress and a federal court case was launched....

**Multinational Monitor: *Let's take milk. Can you tell whether milk has rbGH in it or not?***

**Cummins:** Approximately 10 percent of the fluid milk in the United States today is labeled that it does not have rbGH in it.

But for the 90 percent of the non-organic milk in the United States, consumers are left in the dark as to whether it does contain genetically engineered ingredients. To our knowledge, the only way a consumer can guarantee that processed food or produce is not genetically engineered nowadays is to buy organically certified food.

**Multinational Monitor: *If these foods were labeled as genetically engineered, consumers wouldn't buy them and the technology would be dead.***

**Cummins:** Mandatory labeling, as called for in the May 27, 1998, lawsuit of the Center for Food Safety against the FDA, would slow down the technology to the point where the public could take a long, hard look at it and decide whether it had any benefit or not. As the head of Asgrow Seed Company, now a Monsanto subsidiary, admitted, labeling genetically engineered food in the U.S. would be comparable to putting a skull and crossbones on it.

At this point, the public — even those who don't know that much about this technology — are using common sense and saying, "If industry and government are going to such lengths to conceal from us the fact that they are genetically engineering our food, then it must be dangerous."

**Multinational Monitor: *Do you believe that the technology is dangerous?***

**Cummins:** I believe that it is dangerous, not only to public health but also to the environment. You have to look at each one of the 37 genetically engineered foods and crops individually, but overall genetic engineering creates new toxins, new allergens, damages the nutritional value of food, and creates "superweeds" and "superpests."

This is a totally unnecessary and radical new agricultural technology being rushed to market because these companies want to drive up their stock prices, capture monopoly markets and make more money — not because it is going to do any of things its corporate apologists say, like clean the toxics out of agriculture, or feed the world's hungry....

**Multinational Monitor: *What is your prediction as to the future of genetically engineered foods?***

**Cummins:** Genetically engineered foods are going to fail, just like nuclear power. The kind of opposition that has developed in

Europe and that we are seeing increasing in Japan, Australia and New Zealand is going to spread in the United States. You are going to see the kind of resistance across the board that you saw in 1994 and 1995 against rbGH. We, too, are going to build a mass movement comparable to the anti-nuclear movement of the 1970s and 1980s.

This time it is going to be a mass movement for sustainable and organic agriculture. We will make clear that chemical-intensive and genetically engineered agriculture are a threat to the planet and we have to put an end to them.

READING

# 18

# A HEALTHY REVIEW: rbGH AND HUMAN HEALTH

## U.S. Food and Drug Administration

*The U.S. Food and Drug Administration (FDA) is the regulatory
authority which examines the human health and safety questions
concerning new food and pharmaceutical products ready for market.*

### ■ POINTS TO CONSIDER

1. Identify two reasons the FDA decided to re-review rbGH.

2. Is there a difference if rbGH is orally injested or injected? Explain the FDA's position.

3. Describe the FDA's conclusions on rbGH and a connection to cysts and cancer.

4. According to the FDA, does a significant health risk from antibiotics exist?

5. Evaluate the external review of the FDA's study and conclusions.

Excerpted from the Center for Veterinary Medicine, **"Report on the Food and Drug
Administration's Review of the Safety of Recombinant Bovine Somatotropin,"**
Washington, DC: U.S. Food & Drug Administration, February 1999.

## rbGH can be used without any appreciable risk to the health of consumers.

On November 5, 1993, following extensive review of the data to support the safety and effectiveness of the product, the Food and Drug Administration (FDA or Agency) approved the Monsanto Company's New Animal Drug Application for Posilac containing a recombinant bovine growth hormone (rbGH) (also known as recombinant bovine somatotropin, rbST, or Sometribove).

Growth hormone (GH) is a protein hormone produced in the pituitary gland of animals including humans and is essential for normal growth, development, and health maintenance. Approximately 60 years ago, it was discovered that injecting cows with GH extracted from cattle pituitary glands increased milk production. In the 1980s, it became technically possible and economically feasible to produce large quantities of bovine GH (bGH) using recombinant DNA processes. The Posilac product contains a recombinant bGH (rbGH) which is essentially the same as (pituitary derived) bGH.

In order to grant approval of Posilac, FDA determined, among other things, that food products from cows treated with rbGH are safe for consumption by humans. Vermont Public Interest Research Group and Rural Vermont have questioned the validity of this finding based on an analysis by reviewers at Health Canada (the Canadian counterpart of the FDA). This analysis, based in large part on a 90-day rat study, challenges the Agency's human health findings and argues that possible adverse health effects of Posilac were not addressed because long term toxicology studies to ascertain human health safety were not required by FDA or conducted by Monsanto.

FDA has completed a comprehensive, page by page audit of the human food safety sections of the investigational new animal drug file and master file supporting the rbGH approval. This audit examined all the studies used in determining the human food safety of rbGH, including the 90-day rat oral toxicity study and the report of the antibody response to oral rbGH upon which the Canadian reviewers relied. Upon determining that a review had not been performed of the antibody data during the course of the original review of the Monsanto application, these data were reviewed in their entirety. As set forth in detail below, FDA believes that the Canadian reviewers did not interpret the study results correctly and that there are no new scientific concerns regarding the safety of milk from cows treated with rbGH. The determination that long term studies were not necessary for assessing the safety of rbGH was based on studies which show that: bGH is biologically inactive in humans even if injected, rbGH is orally inactive, and bGH and rbGH are biologically indistinguishable.

## ABSORPTION

When taken orally, proteins typically are broken down in the digestive process and are not absorbed into the body. To determine whether an rbGH product had biologically significant oral activity, the Agency required the drug's sponsor to perform short-term toxicology studies to assess whether biologically active rbGH was being absorbed into the body. Absorption of biologically active rbGH into the body could indicate a need for longer term studies to assess the possible impact on various body organs, particularly the liver. The study was conducted by orally administering rbGH to rats for 28 days at 100 times the daily dose administered to dairy cattle. FDA determined that there was no evidence for the absorption of biologically active rbGH following oral administration because there were no dose-related trends associated with oral administration of rbGH to rats for 28 days.

The Canadian analysis takes issue with the Agency's findings regarding a 90-day rat oral toxicity study performed by Monsanto to fulfill a requirement of the European Union (EU) for rbGH approval. The study was conducted by a Searle laboratory of Monsanto and submitted to FDA pursuant to FDA's requirement that all relevant safety information for an investigational new animal drug be included in the sponsor's application. The FDA reviewed the study in 1989, except as noted below, and it was determined that there were no observed effects from oral administration at any dose. In this study, there was evidence that oral administration of rbGH produced an antibody response; however, such response was consistent with that produced by a number of food proteins and is not necessarily an indication of absorption of intact rbGH.

As rbGH produces significant biological effects when injected into rats, this study supported the inability of rbGH to cause significant biological effects following oral administration even at doses 50 times greater than the injected dose.

The report of the 90-day rat oral toxicity study included discussion of a satellite study group of rats. This satellite study was conducted to investigate the antibody response to rbGH as an indirect measure of the possible absorption of rbGH from the rat gastrointestinal tract. This satellite study was not reviewed when originally submitted.[1] Once this oversight was detected, the Agency immediately undertook the review of the data.

FDA believes that the available data confirm that biologically significant amounts of rbGH are not absorbed in humans following the consumption of milk from cows treated with rbGH. Oral toxicity studies of longer duration are not necessary because rbGH at dietary levels found in the milk of rbGH-treated cows is not significantly biologically available.

## THYROID CYSTS, PROSTATE INFILTRATION

In addition to the antibody results, concern has been raised that the 90-day rat study suggested that rbGH caused the rats to develop thyroid cysts and an infiltration of cells into the prostate. It is argued that such results, if true, would be evidence of absorption of rbGH and possible harmful effects.

An examination of the individual animal reports for gross and histopathological findings revealed thyroid cysts in all treatment groups, including the positive and negative controls.[2] Neither frequency nor severity of these cysts appeared to be related to rbGH

134

administration by either the oral or subcutaneous routes, at any dose, in either gender. Thyroid cysts are enlarged thyroid follicles, and are not related to cancer formation.

A similar examination also was made for the prostate observations. The mononuclear cell infiltration observed is an indication of mild inflammation, and again, is not related to cancer formation. The prostate and accessory sex glands are frequent sites of inflammatory changes in male rats. These changes are common in older rats, but they also occur in young adult rats. Although there appears to be a dose-related increase in the number of rats showing mononuclear cell infiltration following oral administration, there was no difference between the negative and positive control groups. If the prostatic changes were induced by rbGH, it would be expected that the frequency and severity of changes would be significantly greater in the positive versus the negative control group. Therefore, as with the thyroid cysts, these observations do not appear to be related to treatment of the rats with rbGH. Neither the thyroid nor prostate changes provide any evidence of an observable effect of rbGH in the rat and do not provide evidence of absorption.

## IGF-I

The Canadian report indicates that milk from rbGH-treated cows contains significantly elevated levels of insulin-like growth factor I (IGF-I), and presents human health safety concerns. IGF-I is a protein normally found in all humans, and is not intrinsically harmful.

The safety of IGF-I in milk was thoroughly considered by FDA in its review of the Posilac application. Some early studies suggested that treatment of dairy cows with rbGH produced a slight, but statistically significant, increase in the average milk IGF-I concentration. FDA determined that this modest increase in milk IGF-I concentration was not a human food safety concern because it was less than the natural variation in milk IGF-I levels observed during lactation and was less than the fluctuation observed in milk from treated and control cows prior to rbGH administration.

FDA has examined the literature and finds no definitive evidence of any direct link between IGF-I and breast cancer. Some authors have hypothesized a link, whereas others have expressed that while IGF-I is one of several growth factors and hormones that can contribute to an increase in cell numbers of many cell types *in vitro*, no one factor is responsible for changing normal cells into cancerous cells. Furthermore, FDA has been advised that there is no substantive evidence that IGF-I causes normal breast cells to become cancerous.[3]

It bears repeating that the assumptions that milk levels of IGF-I are increased following treatment with rbGH and that biologically active IGF-I is absorbed into the body are not supported by the main body of science. Careful analysis of the published literature fails to provide compelling evidence that milk from rbGH-treated cows contains increased levels of IGF-I compared to milk from untreated cows. Despite recent studies that demonstrate that milk proteins protect IGF-I from digestion, the vast majority of the published work indicates that very little IGF-I is absorbed following ingestion. The most recent 1998 review by the Joint Expert Committee on Food Additives (JECFA) concluded that, "the concentration of IGF-I in milk from rbGH-treated cows is orders of magnitude lower than the physiological amounts produced in the gastrointestinal tract and other parts of the body. Thus, the concentration of IGF-I would not increase either locally in the gastrointestinal tract or systemically, and the potential for IGF-I to promote tumor growth would not increase when milk from rbGH-treated cows was consumed; there is thus no appreciable risk for consumers."

## INFANTS AND CHILDREN

Strong concerns over the potential risk to infants and children from milk containing rbGH were expressed by Vermont Public Interest Group and Rural Vermont but no specific issues were raised to substantiate this concern. The FDA considers the impact on high-risk populations in assessing the safety of new animal drugs. For rbGH in particular, issues related to levels of IGF-I in infant formula were carefully examined by FDA. Other concerns, including the hypothetical development of insulin-dependent diabetes mellitus following the consumption of milk from rbGH-treated cows, have been reviewed by the Agency as well as other national and international scientists. To date, all of these reviews have concluded that consumption by infants and children of milk and edible products from rbGH-treated cows is safe.

## MASTITIS

An August 6, 1992, General Accounting Office (GAO) report found that FDA's review of rbGH had met all established guidelines and that bovine growth hormone did not appear to represent a direct human health risk. However, because rbGH-treated cows tended to have a small but significantly greater incidence of mastitis, GAO recommended that the degree to which antibiotics must be used to treat mastitis should be evaluated in rbGH-treated cows with respect to human food safety. In response to GAO's recommendation, FDA's Center for Veterinary Medicine convened its Veterinary Medicine Advisory Committee and other expert consultants for an open public hearing on March 31, 1993. The Committee concluded that, while rbGH treatment might cause a statistically significant increase in mastitis, the human health risk posed by the possible increased use of antibiotics to treat the mastitis was insignificant. Again, the recent JECFA report addressed the issue of antibiotic use associated with rbGH use. The Committee concluded that "the use of rbGH would not result in a higher risk to human health due to the use of antibiotics to treat mastitis and that the increased potential for drug residues in milk could be managed by practices currently in use within the dairy industry and by following directions for use."

## EXTERNAL REVIEWS

The FDA's review of rbGH has been scrutinized by both the Department of Health and Human Services' Office of Inspector General (OIG) and by GAO, as well as by JECFA. On February 21, 1992, the OIG announced that an audit of issues related to FDA's review of rbGH found no evidence to question FDA's process for determining the human food safety of rbGH. The OIG found that sufficient research had been conducted to substantiate the safety of the milk and meat of rbGH-treated cows for human consumption. In addition, the OIG found no evidence that indicated that FDA or Monsanto engaged in manipulation or suppression of animal health test data. As noted above, the August 6, 1992, GAO report found that FDA's review of rbGH had met all established guidelines and concluded that bovine growth hormone did not pose a risk for human consumption. In its reviews, JECFA also came to the conclusion that rbGH can be used without any appreciable risk to the health of consumers.

# NOTES FOR READING EIGHTEEN

1 Although FDA did not review the antibody data when originally submitted, FDA scientists participated in the discussion of antibody data at the 1992 Joint Food and Agricultural Organization/World Health Organization Expert Committee on Food Additives (JECFA) meeting. The JECFA report states, "Serum somatotropin and rbST antibody production results indicate that orally ingested bST was not absorbed intact from the rat gut at the dose levels tested. Antibody titers slightly higher than background were present in several of the orally-treated rats, but rbST was not detected by RIA [radioimmunoassay]. These data suggest that the immune system has access to an antigenic portion of rbST (Seaman & Skinner, 1986). Formation of antibodies to dietary proteins is a normal response (Bahna & Heiner, 1980: Hammond et al., 1991)." WHO Food Additive Series 31 (1993) Bovine Somatotropins (A Toxicological Evaluation of Certain Veterinary Drug Residues in Food) Annex 1 104:149-165.

2 Rats in the positive control group received rbGH by injection. Rats in the negative control group received no rbGH.

3 Taken from a letter from Dennis M. Bier, M.D., Professor of Pediatrics and Director, Children's Nutrition Research Center, College of Medicine, Baylor University, to David A. Kessler, M.D., Commissioner, Food and Drug Administration, February 25, 1994.

# 19

# DOWN ON THE PHARM

## Justin Gillis

*Justin Gillis is a staff writer at* The Washington Post.

## ■ POINTS TO CONSIDER

1. Why is Rosie the Cow different from other cows?

2. Describe the new biotechnology in animal husbandry.

3. Evaluate the statement "Creating germs with human genes in them is so routine now that it's done in high school laboratories." In light of this, how do you feel about gene modification for animals?

4. Discuss the sundry products made in "bioreactors."

5. How do these cows differ from cows treated with a product of genetic engineering such as rbGH?

***Within a decade or so, there are likely to be thousands of "transgenic" cows...browsing in American pastures, cranking out human proteins in bulk more cheaply than they could be made by any other method.***

On a cold winter morning, a farmhand leads a Holstein cow named Rosie to her trough. She moos. Behind her, the landscape falls way toward a stream lined with sycamore trees. Mountains tower in the distance.

To all appearances, it's a timeless slice of life from a Virginia farm. But looks deceive. Rosie is no ordinary cow, and this is no ordinary farm. It is, instead, a place at the cutting edge of world science. Amid the grunts of pigs and the bleats of hungry calves, the future is taking shape here.

## FACTORIES

The farm is nursery and lab for PPL Therapeutics Inc., the U.S. branch of the company in Scotland whose scientists drew world-wide attention in 1997 when they helped to clone a sheep named Dolly from an adult cell.

While ethicists have been debating human cloning, while legislators have been considering bans and while pastors have been inveighing against tampering with God's creation, PPL scientists have been quietly plugging away in barns and pastures here, trying to sidestep the controversy. They see cloning as a quick, efficient way to produce animals with special genetic traits that can solve health problems, and as a potentially profitable business.

Rosie was created through the artificial manipulation of the very stuff of life. In billions of cells of her body, she carries copies of a human gene. In her milk, she produces a protein that's normally made only by the human body. She was designed to be a factory — or, more precisely, a prototype of a factory — to mass-produce the protein, which can be useful in making drugs. She shows that cows, nature's most prolific producers of milk, can be used to advance medicine.

In a pen next to Rosie lives a year-old bull. His name is Mr. Jefferson. He is an obtuse, slightly dazed critter, not yet old enough to be mean, the way Holstein bulls can get. He doesn't produce milk, of course, but he is there to prove a different point.

140

## TRANSGENIC AND CLONED ANIMALS

Mr. Jefferson, born on Presidents' Day 1998 and named for Virginia's favorite son, is a clone. He was created from a cell of a cow fetus. The point he proves is that the scientists working on this farm can clone cattle, giving them greater control over genetic alterations — and the ability, if they want, to create a herd of identical animals in short order.

Up the hill from Rosie and Mr. Jefferson live some pigs. Like pigs anywhere, they stink. But three of them are special, containing genetic modifications that may make their organs a bit more like those of human beings. Some day, the people who run this place envision growing thousands of genetically modified pigs whose lives would be sacrificed so that their hearts and kidneys could be transplanted into sick people. If it works, this technique would solve the shortage of organs for transplant, saving lives.

Already, hundreds of genetically engineered PPL sheep in Scotland are turning out a human protein called alpha-1-antitrypsin in their milk. The sheep were produced by an earlier method, not by cloning, but they are special nevertheless. Alpha-1-antitrypsin from sheep's milk, impossible to produce in sufficient quantity by any other method, is undergoing tests on humans as a potential treatment for cystic fibrosis, a life-threatening lung disease.

Sheep are good for producing some drugs, and so are rabbits. But for proteins likely to be needed in large quantity, cows are likely to be the best factories....

## ROUTINE PRACTICE TO APPLICATION

Within a decade or so, there are likely to be thousands of "transgenic" cows like Rosie browsing in American pastures, cranking out human proteins in bulk more cheaply than they could be made by any other method. Most of those proteins will be given to people as treatments to fight hemophilia and other diseases.

PPL is one of three major biotechnology companies, and several smaller ones, pursuing these techniques. People who work at these companies often say they're "pharming," using animals to produce drugs. At least three drugs produced this way already have been given to people in tests. In short, these companies are busy creating an industry unlike any other....

Since the 1970s scientists have been manipulating DNA to create new forms of life, and today it's a growing for-profit business. To date, the manipulations have been carried out mostly in single-celled organisms or in mammal cells that will grow vigorously in a nutrient broth. One of the earliest achievements was to take the gene for human insulin, the protein that controls blood sugar, and insert it into germs. These germs were then induced to make large quantities of insulin. The lives of many diabetics now depend on insulin made this way.

Creating germs with human genes in them is so routine now that it's done in high school science laboratories. Numerous biotechnology companies perform such manipulations, searching for commercially valuable proteins.

The technology works. But it is costly, requiring sterile rooms, highly trained technicians and huge vats called "bioreactors." So biotechnologists have begun looking to nature's most efficient producer of proteins, the breasts of female mammals.

Hence the farm in Blacksburg....

## HUMAN NEEDS

Close to two dozen cows and calves on the farm are carrying human genes. Rosie, 2 1/2, is the oldest. In her milk, she produces a human protein called alpha lactalbumin, likely to be useful someday as a nutritional supplement for babies and the elderly. Indeed, one eventual goal of the research is to produce cow's milk that more closely resembles human milk, on the theory that it would be healthier for people to drink.

Counting what's come from the milk of mice, rabbits, sheep and cows, PPL scientists have managed to produce more than 30 human proteins and are working to develop 11 of them. Now the company is trying to settle on a protein to produce in bulk, which might take place by cloning a bunch of factory animals.

One candidate is a clotting factor needed by hemophiliacs. That protein already is used as a drug, but it is produced from donated human blood. That's an expensive proposition; it's also plagued by the ever-present fear of contamination if new viruses get into the blood supply, as the AIDS virus did in the 1980s.

Another possibility is alpha-1-antitrypsin. It can already be produced from human blood, and Bayer Corp., the pharmaceutical giant, does so in order to treat people who are genetically deficient in the protein. Without treatment, they are afflicted by life-threatening emphysema. Yet the protein is expensive to produce from blood, is in chronically short supply and is largely unavailable outside the United States.

PPL now is making this protein in a flock of sheep in Scotland, where it has built a factory to purify the drug, and may eventually make it in cows in the United States. This has vastly expanded the supply and has allowed the company to target a new, far larger group that may benefit from the drug. These are people who have cystic fibrosis, which usually chops decades off the lives of people it strikes. About 30,000 Americans suffer from cystic fibrosis, and many of them die as teenagers.

## SAFE IN THE ENVIRONMENT

Small-scale tests of alpha-1-antitrypsin in cystic fibrosis patients in Britain have yielded hopeful results, and PPL has just begun testing in a handful of people in the United States. The transplantation of foreign genes into plants has provoked widespread fear around the world that mankind would poison the environment. But to date there has been less concern about transgenic livestock, in part because the reproduction of animals, unlike that of field crops, can be tightly controlled. Transgenic animals are so valuable — they can cost millions of dollars apiece to create — that they are not likely to be turned loose willy-nilly into the environment....

# INTERPRETING EDITORIAL CARTOONS

*This activity may be used as an individualized study guide for students in libraries and resource centers or as a discussion catalyst in small group and classroom discussions.*

Although cartoons are usually humorous, the main intent of most political cartoonists is not to entertain. Cartoons express serious social comment about important issues. Using graphics and visual arts, the cartoonist expresses opinions and attitudes. By employing an entertaining and often light-hearted visual format, cartoonists may have as much or more impact on national and world issues as editorial and syndicated columnists.

## Points to Consider

1. Examine the cartoon in Reading Seventeen.

2. How would you interpret the message of the cartoon?
   Try to describe the message in one to three sentences.

3. Do you agree with the message expressed in the cartoon?
   Why or why not?

4. Are any readings in Chapter Three in basic agreement with this cartoon?

5. Does the cartoon support the author's point of view in any of the readings in this book? If the answer is yes, be specific about which reading or readings and why.

# BIBLIOGRAPHY

Agricultural Economics and Technology: Proceedings of the Conference Held at Biotech 87, London, May 1987 (World Biotech Report 1987, Vol. 1, Part 4) Online Pubns. June 1987.

Aldridge, Susan, **The Thread of Life: The Story of Genes and Genetic Engineering,** Cambridge [England]; New York, NY, USA: Cambridge University Press, 1996.

Anderson, Water Truett, **Evolution Isn't What It Used to Be: The Augmented Animal and the Whole Wired World,** New York: W.H. Freeman, 1996.

Appleyard, Bryan, **Brave New Worlds: Staying Human in the Genetic Future,** New York: Viking, 1998.

Beck-Gernsheim, Elisabeth, **The Social Implications of Bioengineering,** Atlantic Highlands, N.J.: Humanities Press, 1995.

Berg, Paul, **Dealing with Genes: The Language of Heredity,** Mill Valley: University Science Books, 1992.

**Biotechnology: Science, Engineering, and Ethical Challenges for the Twenty-First Century** / Frederick B. Rudolph and Larry V. McIntire, editors, Washington, D.C.: Joseph Henry Press, 1996.

Bryan, Jenny, **Genetic Engineering,** New York: Thomson Learning, 1995.

Cohen, Robert, **Milk: The Deadly Poison,** Englewood Cliffs, NJ: Argus Publishing, 1998.

Darling, David J., **Genetic Engineering: Redrawing the Blueprint of Life,** Parsippany, NJ: Dillon Press, 1995.

Deane-Drummond, Celia, **Theology and Biotechnology: Implications for a New Science,** London; Washington: Geoffrey Chapman, 1997.

Drlica, Karl, **Double-Edged Sword: the Promises and Risks of the Genetic Revolution,** Reading, Mass.: Addison-Wesley, c1994.

Emery, Alan E.H., **An Introduction to Recombinant DNA,** Chichester [Sussex]; New York: Wiley, c1984.

Fincham, J.R.S., **Genetically Engineered Organisms: Benefits and Risks,** Toronto: University of Toronto Press, 1991.

Fox, Michael W., **Animals Have Rights, Too,** Continuum, 1991.

Gros, Francois, **The Gene Civilization,** McGraw Hill, 1992.

Halvorson, H.O. (editor) & Gal, Y. Le, **New Developments in Marine Biotechnology,** Plenum Pub Corp., July 1998.

Harris, John, **Wonderwoman and Superman: The Ethics of Human Biotechnology,** Oxford [England]; New York: Oxford University Press, 1992.

Howard, Ted, **Who Should Play God? The Artificial Creation of Life and What It Means for the Future of the Human Race,** Delacorte Press, 1977.

Hynes, Patricia H., **The Recurring Silent Spring,** Pergamon Press, 1989.

Kimbrell, Andrew, **The Human Body Shop: The Engineering and Marketing of Life,** 1st Harper Collins pbk. ed., San Francisco: Harper San Francisco, 1994.

Kornberg, Arthur, **The Golden Helix: Inside Biotech Ventures,** University Science Books, May 1996. Olive Hill Lane Press.

Krattiger, Anatole F., **The Importance of Ag-Biotech to Global Prosperity (ISAAA Briefs),** Intl. Serv. for the Acquisition of Agri-biotech Apps., May 1, 1998.

Lee, Thomas F., **Gene Future, The Promise and Perils of the New Biology,** New York: Plenum Press, 1993.

Liebhardt, William C., **The Dairy Debate: Consequences of Bovine Growth Hormone and Rotational Grazing Technologies,** Davis, CA: University of California Sustainable Agriculture Research and Education Programs, 1993.

Mather, Robin, **A Garden of Unearthly Delights: Bioengineering and the Future of Food,** New York: Dutton, 1995.

Mass Market Paperback, **High Tech Survival: The Impact of Government on High Tech and BioTech Companies,** Olive Hill Lane Press, October 1996.

McCuen, Gary E., **Manipulating Life: Debating the Genetic Revolution,** GEM, 1985.

Moses, V., **Exploiting Biotechnology,** Australia; United States: Harwood Academic Publishers, c1995.

Murrell, J.C., **Understanding Genetic Engineering,** Halsted Press, 1989.

Oliver, Richard W., **The Coming Biotech Age: The Business of Bio-Materials,** McGraw-Hill, January 1999.

Prentls, Steve, **Biotechnology: A New Industrial Revolution,** New York: G. Braziller, 1984.

Raeburn, Paul, **The Last Harvest: The Genetic Gamble that Threatens to Destroy American Agriculture,** New York: Simon & Schuster, 1995.

Reiss, Michael J., **Improving Nature? The Science and Ethics of Genetic Engineering,** New York: Cambridge University Press, 1996.

Rifkin, Jeremy, **Declaration of a Heretic,** Boston: Routledge & Kegan Paul, 1985.

Rifkin, Jeremy, **The Biotech Century: Harnessing the Gene and Remaking the World,** J.P. Tarcher, 1999.

Russo, V.E.A. (Vincenzo E.A.), **Genetic Engineering: Dreams and Nightmares,** Oxford; New York: Oxford University Press, 1998.

Shapiro, Robert, **The Human Blueprint: The Race to Unlock the Secrets of Our Genetic Script,** St. Martins Press, 1991.

Silver, Lee M., **Remaking Eden: Cloning and Beyond in a Brave New World,** New York Avon Books, 1997.

Sofer, William H., **Introduction to Genetic Engineering,** Boston: Butterworth-Heinemann, c1991.

Spallone, Patricia, **Generation Games: Genetic Engineering and the Future for Our Lives,** Philadelphia: Temple University Press, c1992.

Stwertka, Eve, **Genetic Engineering,** F. Watts, 1989.

Swisher, Clarice, **Genetic Engineering,** San Diego: Lucent Books, 1996.

Tagliaferro, Linda, **Genetic Engineering: Progress or Peril?** Minneapolis: Lerner Publications, 1997.

Todd, Nancy Jack, **Bioshelters, Oceans, Arks, City Farming: Ecology as the Basis of Design,** Sierra Club Books, 1984.

Tudge, Colin, **The Engineer in the Garden: Genes and Genetics: From the Idea of Heredity to the Creation of Life,** New York: Hill and Wang, 1995, 1993.

Wells, Donna K., **Biotechnology,** New York: Benchmark Books, 1996.

Williams, J.G., **Genetic Engineering,** IRL Press, 1988.

Yount, Lisa, **Genetics and Genetic Engineering,** New York: Facts on File, 1997.

Yoxen, Edward, **The Gene Business: Who Should Control Biotechnology?** New York: Oxford University Press, 1986, c1983.


**General Web Sites:**

http://www.ebi.ac.uk/

http://www.isinet.com/

http://net.bio.net/

http://www.er.doe.gov/production/ober/bioinfo_center.html

http://www.ornl.gov/hgmis/

http://cdnseed.org/othersit.html

http://www.cts.com/crash/publish/century.html

http://biotech.icmb.utexas.edu/pages/tools.html

http://www.bio.org/welcome.html (best)

http://www.geneletter.org/ (very good)

http://www.bioinfo.com/

**Human Genome:**

http://www.ncgr.org/

http://www.ncbi.nlm.nih.gov/SCIENCE96/

http://www.nhgri.nih.gov/ (best)

**Journals:**

http://www.bio.org/links/journals.html (links)

**Timeline:**

http://www.bio.org/timeline/timeline.html

**Corporate Lists:**

http://www.bio.org/aboutbio/biomembers.html

**Government:**

http://www.epa.gov/opptintr/biotech/index.html

http://www.nal.usda.gov/bic/

http://www.aphis.usda.gov/

http://bioethics.gov/cgi-bin/bioeth_counter.pl

**Online Magazines:**

http://www.recap.com/

**Groups online:**

http://www.biotactics.com/news.htm

**News Groups:**

bionet.announce

bionet.biophysics

bionet.cellbiol

bionet.genome.arabidopsis

bionet.genome.autosequencing

bionet.genome.chromosomes

bionet.immunology

bionet.jobs.offered

bionet.molbio.evolution

bionet.molbio.genbank.updates

bionet.molbio.hiv

bionet.molbio.methds-reagnts

bionet.molbio.proteins

bionet.molbio.yeast

bionet.toxicology

bionet.virology

bionet.women-in-bio

clari.biz.industry.agriculture

clari.biz.industry.health

clari.biz.industry.health.pharma

clari.tw.health

clari.tw.health.aids

clari.tw.science+space

misc.jobs.fields.chemistry

sci.bio.botany

sci.bio.food-science

sci.bio.microbiology

sci.bio.technology

sci.chem

sci.engr.biomed

sci.med.immunology

sci.med.informatics

sci.med.pharmacy

sci.research

sci.research.careers

sci.research.postdoc

sci.techniques.microscopy

# INDEX